THE *DESPICABLE* MISSIONARY

How a young Christian girl in Pakistan learned to defend her faith and love Muslims

Annie Bradley with Julie Dass

"Look at it this way: At the right time, while we were still helpless, Christ died for ungodly people. Finding someone who would die for a godly person is rare. Maybe someone would have the courage to die for a good person. Christ died for us while we were still sinners.

"This demonstrates God's love for us. Since Christ's blood has now given us God's approval, we are even more certain that Christ will save us from God's anger.

"If the death of his Son restored our relationship with God while we were still his enemies, we are even more certain that, because of this restored relationship, the life of his Son will save us.

"In addition, our Lord Jesus Christ lets us continue to brag about God. After all, it is through Christ that we now have this restored relationship with God."

St. Paul's letter to the Romans, 5:6-11, GWT

Copyright © 2017 Mission Nation Publishing

All rights reserved
ISBN: 0996677984
ISBN 13: 9780996677981
Mission Nation Publishing, Naples, Fl.

LETTER FROM A PASTOR

I first met *Victoria and her husband* in December 2011 when they walked into Faith Lutheran Church for worship. They had come to learn more of what Faith Lutheran was about, and wanted to hear the Word of God. It was at that moment that their love for mission became clear to me.

Victoria shared from her heart her desire to visit Lutheran churches throughout our denomination and share how God is working to reach men and women of the Eastern cultures and religions. It was refreshing to meet someone who wanted to see God transform lives of men and women from darkness and fear to faith, grace, love, and freedom in Jesus Christ; her desire also was to encourage fellow Christians to be strong and courageous in defending the Gospel.

She took as her life example the teaching ministry of the Lord Jesus Christ. She saw how He would reach out to all communities and then demonstrate His love for them. This is how she now lives out her life.

Now, five years later, we have enjoyed seeing *Victoria*'s personal faith, and the mission she leads, touch so many human hearts. She has been a leader in helping others see the importance of sharing the Gospel with Muslims, Hindus, and Sikhs.

On a more personal level, this has been even more direct. Over the past years, Victoria has sung the Psalms in Urdu and played her Pakistani drum at my son's and daughter's weddings; she has served me hundreds of meals of Pakistani dishes, and, most important, she has shown how, in Bible Study classes, it is possible to have mission integrated into every facet of our congregation's corporate life.

Thank you, Victoria. As God's love has changed your life, you have changed ours for the better.

Pastor Don Treglown

NOTE FROM THE PUBLISHER

What was it like to grow up as a Christian, more, as a girl Christian, in Pakistan? It was to be called *"paleed,"* "despicable."

How do you not get angry at everyone? How do you love your neighbor, and live a life of love and forgiveness in a society that works hard to show how much it despises you?

This story is true. It happened. It is happening to many. Christians believe God is love, and loved this world, and entered the world. Jesus was despicable to the people of His time. Jesus is with us now, in the community of faith that loves, even when it is persecuted. God loves the despicable.

That is what this book is about.

CONTRIBUTORS TO THIS EDITION

Mission Nation Publishing is grateful to the many people who worked on The Despicable Missionary: the author, Annie Bradley and Julie Dass, the co-author. Todd Luedtke put in endless hours editing the manuscript, and he did it as a volunteer. Elizabeth Burke volunteered many hours of her time proofreading.

Most of all, thanks are due to Victoria – who was brave enough to tell her story; her voice will now be heard.

Mission Nation Publishing exists *"To give a voice to the Missionaries to America."* There are many others who have courageous stories to tell. You can see video interviews of some of them at:

www.MisisonNationPublishing.org

TABLE OF CONTENTS

Letter from a Pastor   iii
Note from the Publisher   v
Contributors to this Edition   vii
Prologue   xi

Chapter 1   "Despicable"   1
Chapter 2   "A Father's Lesson"   7
Chapter 3   "The Outcast"   12
Chapter 4   "She Is a Child, Just Like You"   18
Chapter 5   "The Gifts of Christmas"   23
Chapter 6   "Sangla School"   27
Chapter 7   "There Are Consequences for Your Actions"   34
Chapter 8   "Disgrace"   48
Chapter 9   "A New Opportunity"   53
Chapter 10   "An Unexpected Acceptance"   57
Chapter 11   "My Brother"   61
Chapter 12   "An Unexpected Invitation"   67
Chapter 13   "A Bridge Is Begun"   71
Chapter 14   "Building the Bridge"   75
Chapter 15   "Nationalization"   79
Chapter 16   "The Protests Begin"   85
Chapter 17   "Pursuit"   90

Chapter 18	"Whom Can We Trust?"	98
Chapter 19	"An Attempt at Conversion"	105
Chapter 20	"An Offense"	114
Chapter 21	"A Faith Mission Revealed"	118
Chapter 22	"In Mourning"	124
Chapter 23	"A Missionary"	127
Chapter 23	"The Cross I Cannot Refuse"	140
Chapter 24	"An Unknown Brother"	144
Chapter 25	"The Lost Sheep"	148
Chapter 26	"The Strength to Forgive"	151
Chapter 27	"Independence Day"	158
Chapter 28	"Judgment"	164
Chapter 29	"Her Voice of Faith"	173

PROLOGUE

Talib Syed approached his father's home, one leaden foot following the other, the burden of his decision a heavy weight on his shoulders. He knew what he had done was unforgivable, at least in his father's eyes, but at the same time he knew it was for his own good, and that of his wife and children. He prayed he would be met with a small measure of forgiveness from his father. He had little hope.

When he entered his father's home, where he lived along with his wife and children, he greeted his wife first. He pulled her to an empty corner, out of earshot of everyone else.

"I am going to tell father now," Talib told her. Though she said nothing, her eyes widened in concern. "We will plan to meet at the farm down the street after everyone is asleep, just like we've talked about. Promise you will come."

She nodded her assent and slipped away without a word. He assumed she'd begun to pack some necessities for the children. What he'd asked of her, to sneak away in the middle of the night, towing along three tired children, would be a monumental task. They both knew the risks, but for a life that was better for them, and for their family, they'd accept those challenges.

Talib approached his father in the *bethak*. Here the two men could discuss Talib's decision, away from their wives and the children. Alone, in case their conversation became heated and disruptive.

"Father," Talib said quietly.

"Hello my son." His father folded the newspaper he was reading and placed it in his lap.

"We must talk."

"Of course," Talib's brows knitted in concern. "What is on your mind?"

"I've made a decision. You may not agree with it or understand it, but I pray you will respect it."

Talib took a deep breath. He looked down at his hands that were clasped together, moist with perspiration. He searched deep within himself to relay his news in a way to keep his father's respect. Talib recalled the words he'd read from the book Major John had gifted to him, words that brought him peace and comfort, knowledge and joy, like no other book he had read before. He took another deep breath, and with a prayer of thanksgiving, he surrendered himself to Jesus Christ.

"I've become a Christian, father."

Talib felt the love of the Holy Spirit wash over him and wrap him within its grace. Filled with love and peace, Talib lifted his head and looked at his father. Daggers of hatred shot from his father's eyes and quickly gave way to a look of utter disgust. Talib had never seen his father look at him in such a way. His father's eyes had always looked at him with love and pride, until this moment. Despite that, Talib knew his choice was the right one.

"Surely you jest, Talib. It is a cruel joke," his father spat.

"It is not a joke, father. I have made my choice."

"I never should have allowed you to join that army. The British? The infidels? They've poisoned your mind, Talib. How can you be so weak? After all I've taught you."

His father jumped up from the chair, the movement lithe, in denial of his true age. He advanced on Talib, shouting, as he poked a finger into Talib's chest. Talib backed into a wall, but he did not cower at the wrath of his father. The Holy Spirit gave him the strength to remain strong.

"I will take my family and we will leave, father. Clearly, you are unable to respect my choice. For a man so faithful, I thought more of you than this. I thought the teachings of the *Quran* would have made you more open minded."

Talib puffed his chest and stood taller. He would not recoil or feel shame about his conversion to Christ.

"You will leave your family here. At least they can remain a valued part of the Muslim community. They don't need to be shamed because of you."

His father balled his fists. Talib was fearful that his father would strike him, something he'd never done before.

"I am not ashamed father." Talib said. "I am filled with the love of Jesus Christ and the Holy Spirit."

"Shut your filthy mouth!" his father bellowed. "You are no longer my son. If I ever see you again, I will kill you!"

"How can you consider yourself a holy man when hatred comes so easily to you?" Talib asked quietly. Now he retreated, trying to keep his body from shaking. He couldn't understand how he could be adored by his father for his entire life but in one moment become so deeply hated.

"You are dead to me." Talib's father turned his back on his son. Their conversation was over. These would be the last words ever exchanged between father and son.

Without a word, Talib turned on his heel and left the house with the knowledge that he'd never see his parents again. When he reached the end of the street, out of sight of the home where he'd lived all his life, he allowed his tears to flow. He mourned the respect he would never again have from his father. He mourned the fact that his father, and by association his mother, would never be able to find forgiveness and love in their hearts to accept their son as a Christian, even though he was the same person he'd always been. Overwhelmed with grief, Talib sat under an oak tree, and wept.

In the still of night, Talib waited among the overgrown vegetation of the farm down the road where he and his wife had agreed to meet. He'd prayed all day that Jesus would give his wife the strength and courage to meet him. The sun had set hours ago, and the darkest part of the night was upon them. With a heavy heart, Talib began to give up hope. There was no sign of his family.

Just as he convinced himself it was time to take leave of the village, he heard rustling through the thick dead stalks where he'd hidden himself. His eldest son burst through the foliage. *"Papa!"* he shouted in delight.

"Hush, hush," Talib commanded through his tears of happiness as he pulled the young boy into a great embrace.

Soon his wife appeared, their third child, Ishaq, asleep in a basket on top of the few meager belongings his wife collected from Talib's father's home. She carried their middle son on her hip, and another child within her womb. Talib grabbed her face in his hands and pressed a kiss to her forehead. When he pulled from her, she gave him a bright, yet tired, smile.

Talib's prayers had been answered. He'd heard the call of Jesus Christ and accepted him joyfully in his heart. With his wife and children by his side, Talib Syed could begin his true life's journey. This journey would not be an easy one. Talib and his family would be met with religious persecution because of his conversion to Christianity. He prayed he would find the strength to meet any religious prejudice he encountered with love and understanding. He strove to integrate that into what he taught his children and hoped that the generations that followed would learn to replace their hatred with love.

CHAPTER 1

"DESPICABLE"

"She is *paleed!*" a young boy named Nafees screamed, his accusing finger pointed at Victoria as she and a neighborhood girl both sat on the shiny new red tricycle her parents had bought for her. The acquisition of such a rare and expensive plaything made Victoria's house a destination for the neighborhood children. All of them were eager for Victoria to allow them a turn and Victoria was willing. She and some of the neighborhood boys and girls had taken turns pedaling up and down the street for a good hour. Until now.

The little girl who shared the tricycle's seat with Victoria, slowly stood. She backed away, her brown eyes wide as if she'd just discovered she'd been playing with a rattle snake dressed as a little girl.

"*Paleed!*" "Despicable." Nafees yelled again, a warning to the Muslim children who'd been duped into playing with Victoria, the glamour of the red tricycle too much to resist. The children who'd been playing either backed away or took off running as fast as they could in the direction of their homes.

"She's *paleed* and you're riding on her cycle!"

Victoria's sweet face curled into a scowl, her fists balled up and her face flushed with rage.

1

"What did you say?" she asked the boy, staring coldly into his eyes from her seat on the tricycle. His mouth opened in a circle of surprise at Victoria's challenge, but he wasn't taken off guard for long. Nafees crossed his arms and stared back at her with a mixture of hatred and disgust; a disturbingly mature combination of emotions for a young boy of six years old.

"You are *paleed*," he said with venom. "You are not like us. You are dirty. Now everyone knows."

Victoria leapt from her tricycle, knocking it onto its side in the dusty, unpaved street. She stomped toward him, her fists still balled, her eyes narrowed. The little boy held his ground, firm in his belief that Victoria was indeed *paleed*. *Paleed* means despicable, unclean or impure; it is one of the most hurtful insults anyone could hurl at a child in Pakistan. He called her *paleed* because she was a Christian.

Victoria's left fist connected with his nose. Her right socked Nafees in the belly. As he crumpled to the ground, sobbing, Victoria hopped on top of him; left, right, left, right she punched, no longer hearing the shouts of the children who had lingered. She didn't feel the softness of his face beneath her fists, or feel the crunch of the cartilage in his nose. She didn't care, she continued to punch.

She was hitting away insults and the pain she endured at being called *paleed*. Again. It was no different in this city than it had been in the others where she'd lived in Pakistan.

Suddenly, a hand grasped the back of Victoria's dress, near the neckline, and she was pulled from on top of the little boy and tossed to the street. Her feet crumpled beneath her and she landed hard on her hip. The little boy she'd beaten was left in the middle of the street, smears of dirt along both of his cheeks and rivulets of blood trickling from his nose.

"Victoria, what are you doing?"

Her mother's shrill voice cut through the village streets. Victoria's pain at being insulted in such a harsh way, subsided long enough for her to realize she would now be in trouble for hitting this young boy.

"Go, stand by the front door," her mother demanded, a long thin finger pointing Victoria in the direction she was to go. Victoria headed toward the front gate of their home, after her mother gave a gentle push to her back.

As she walked toward the family home, fury still knotted in her belly, Victoria turned to look behind her and glared at the boy who had dared insult her. Nafees ran crying to his mother who had rushed toward him. Victoria saw her mother's shoulders slump, as she walked toward Nafees's mother. Her mother's hands were clasped prayerfully together in apology, but the boy's mother scooped her son up into her arms and held him tight. She glowered at Victoria's mother, the narrow set to her jaw indicated she was not going to accept any apology that was offered.

Victoria sat on the front stoop, arms crossed, feet planted firmly on the dusty ground, a scowl rooted on her face. Occasionally she'd make eye contact with the few scattered children who had remained during the altercation between Victoria and Nafees. The children were making their way back toward their homes, now that the thrashing was over. Victoria caught the eye one boy who wore a dirty blue shirt. He'd been the first boy to approach Victoria, the first boy she allowed a turn on her tricycle. He turned his head away when their eyes met and quickened his pace from a walk to a run as he made his way toward home.

When you are young, the several minute conversation Victoria's mother had with Nafees's mother seemed like an eternity. Finally, her mother walked back toward her daughter, her mother's mouth pressed together, and her eyes narrowed. Her back was straight as a pin and she walked swiftly toward her daughter.

"Come here," she demanded harshly. "You will go and apologize to that boy for hitting him and tell him you forgive him for calling you names." Victoria opened her mouth to protest. "You will apologize," her mother said, her tone stern, her eyes angry.

Victoria walked over to Nafees and his mother, dragging her feet.

Victoria swallowed hard and willed the words to come out: "I am sorry for hitting you," she muttered.

"And," her mother prompted.

"He called me names!" she insisted.

"Victoria!" her mother hissed.

"I forgive you for calling me names," Victoria said through clenched teeth.

"Thank you for your apology," the boy's mother said in a flat tone. It seemed to Victoria she only accepted the apology out of obligation and not because she wanted to. Nafees still sniffed back tears, his face hidden in his mother's *gameez*.

"Is he going to apologize to me?" Victoria asked.

"Victoria!" her mother cried, exasperated.

"Why doesn't he have to apologize? He did something wrong, too!"

"Go in the house," her mother ordered firmly. *"Now!"* Victoria stomped her feet the whole way back to her family home, this time not looking back.

Victoria and her family lived in a home in the city of Khanewal, subsidized by the government as a perk of her father's job. Because he worked for the government, they moved from city to city as his job demanded. While moving was often cumbersome and unwelcome, the government took care of its employees by providing them with upper-class, European style homes. Victoria's family was often moved into housing built by the British for their high ranking military officers during the British occupation of Pakistan through World War II. Unlike traditional homes in Pakistan, these were made of brick, well insulated to keep the home cool from the sweltering heat and stifling humidity that often struck the country throughout the year.

Victoria's mother led her into the great room, the main room of the house where everyone would gather to relax, to eat and to sleep. As was the custom in Pakistan, they sat off the floor, on the charpai, facing one another. Victoria found it difficult to meet her mother's eyes.

"Victoria, why did you beat that little boy?" she asked.

Victoria's mouth curled into a petulant pout and she crossed her arms in defiance. "He called me *paleed*." Victoria spat the word out with venom. Her mother sighed.

"Victoria, you are not allowed to hurt someone like that when they say mean things to you."

"He hurt my feelings. He said no one wanted to play with me anymore. All the other kids went away. They didn't think I was un-clean when they wanted to play with my tricycle, but once Nafees called me *paleed*, they all believed him. Why?" Victoria asked, tears welling in her eyes.

"Victoria, we are Christian, we are different," her mother said. "And sometimes, people can't understand or accept those differ-ences. So, we must learn to turn the other cheek, just like the Bible says."

"Why should people be mad at us because we are Christian?"

Her mother sighed. "Because they don't understand and they don't want to. It's best just to be forgiving; that's what Jesus would teach us to do."

"It's not nice to be mad at us because we are different from them. The Bible says we should be good to everyone."

"I know, Victoria, and we should be nice to everyone. That's why we don't hit or hurt others when they hurt our feelings," her mother said, taking both of Victoria's small hands in her large ones.

"We must be the best people we can; the nicest people we can be. What others think we are doesn't matter. If we are the best that we can be, Jesus knows it, and it's what He thinks that really matters, isn't it?"

Victoria stared at her hands still held by her mother's. "I guess." She snuck a glance at her mother, whose face remained firm and impassive. "I mean, yes," Victoria quickly amended.

"Good," her mother said, enveloping her in a bear hug. "Now, go outside and get your tricycle and bring it into the courtyard."

Victoria did as her mother asked. She righted the tricycle from its upturned spot in the street. The once shiny new tricycle, that had attracted so many potential neighborhood friends, was covered in dust and stone from the roadway. The newness of the bike was worn away, and the potential that it brought just as tarnished. She wheeled it into the courtyard and abandoned it near the fountain where her two younger sisters played with their dolls. She turned back toward the house knowing she'd never again get the same enjoyment from the very expensive toy her parents had gotten for her. She retreated to a corner of the great room with her favorite picture book, and lost herself in the story.

CHAPTER 2

"A FATHER'S LESSON"

At dinner that night, Ishaq and his family sat in the great room upon a long white sheet. They had sturdy caned chairs with brightly colored embroidered cushions on which to sit, but, as was the custom in Pakistan, they sat on the floor for their evening meal.

A wooden plate woven with bright triangles of red, green and yellow straw held the *chapati*, or flat bread, and was passed around for everyone to take a piece. Mother had made the *chapati* tonight, so it was still warm and fresh from the *tava*, the flat pan she used to cook the bread. Her mother, Susan, scooped *biryani* into each bowl. She noticed Victoria's scowl when the bowl was placed in front of her.

The children greedily ripped small sections of *chapati* from the larger hunk they'd taken and scooped up the curried rice dish. A pungent smell arose from the chicken cooked in a potpourri of spices: cardamom, onion, garlic, cloves, cinnamon and coriander. With a second hunk of bread, they dipped it into the bowl of *raita*, a yogurt mixed with cucumber and mint. It helped to soothe their palates from the heat of the spices. Yet while her siblings ate with zest, Victoria picked at her meal.

"You aren't yourself tonight, Victoria," her father said. He put down his cup of chai tea and turned toward her. His wife excused herself and went to the kitchen to retrieve the plate of fresh fruit she had prepared for dessert.

Victoria merely shrugged and pushed her bowl away. She would not meet her father's eyes. Her guilt was obvious.

Ishaq sighed. "Do you want to tell me what happened today?"

"Don't you know already?" she asked.

A slight smile touched his lips. He hoped his daughter hadn't noticed. "I do, but I'd like to hear it from you."

"Why did that boy call me *paleed*? I'm not despicable, Father, I'm Christian." Tears welled in Victoria's almond shaped brown eyes and threatened to slide down her cheeks.

Victoria's father worked as a sub-divisional officer for the government. Often his job entailed mediating disputes between farmers over irrigation. While he was excellent at his job, and a masterful peace keeper, Victoria's personality was the opposite of his. Instead of turning the other cheek as Christians are taught, Victoria fought back.

While her father often told Victoria that he admired her strength of character and determination, he found it nearly impossible to break through her petulance and teach her to consider her actions before responding with force. Her actions today could impact the peace they'd found living in this city. Many of the people whom they lived among were people her father worked with. While it was widely known that they were a Christian family, Ishaq's position as peace keeper could have been compromised by his daughter's outburst.

A Muslim man may not take kindly to any advice offered by a common Christian man; Christians are considered unclean by many Pakistani Muslims. A Christian man of Ishaq's social status was uncommon; more respect was shown to the educated Pakistani Christians.

"Victoria, sometimes it is difficult for people to accept or understand those who are different from themselves. As Christians, we are of a different zat than our Muslim brothers and sisters. And that's okay. As Christians, we must learn to forgive them for what they cannot understand."

(The caste system in Pakistan divides society into degrees of ritual purity and social status. S*yed* Muslims are considered the highest caste. Christians, who often have less desirable jobs such as maids or trash collectors, hold the lowest caste, and are believed to be unholy.)

"Grandfather says only dogs and cats have a zat." Victoria retorted. "He says we are human beings and our family follows Jesus Christ. That's all that should matter."

Victoria lowered her eyes in respect whenever she quoted her grandfather. Ishaq knew that Victoria had always felt a profound closeness to her grandfather, a bond beyond what she'd felt with anyone else; his father had a profound influence on her faith.

Ishaq couldn't help himself; he smiled when he heard his father's words echoed through his young child. His father, Talib, was a respected man, well-educated and grounded in the Christian faith. Whenever he was with the children, he made sure to teach them the ways of Christ. Victoria listened to him with rapt attention.

"Grandfather's point of view is not wrong," Ishaq said, treading carefully.

What a delicate balance he had to navigate with his daughter. He wanted to retain her innocence, allow her to believe she could be who she was and the world would accept her. Soon enough, Pakistan would try to teach her differently.

Few Muslims, even the most devout, did not treat Christians well.

In Pakistan, Christians were lower class citizens. It was part of the reason Ishaq struggled not to stir up trouble between Christians and Muslims. There was no need to shout it from the mountains and risk their lives. Some radicalized Muslim sects would hunt out Christians, to hurt and disgrace them. This was what worried Ishaq for his fearless daughter. We are thankful for our Christian faith."

He plucked a date from the plate of fruit his wife had placed next to him.

"If we are asked, we should never deny who we are, but we don't need to go out of our way to say so." He popped the date into his mouth, to indicate to Victoria that their conversation was over.

When the fruit plate was passed to her, she chose a ripe slice of mango. The juices rolled down her hand as she took a bite. The delicious fruit seemed to quiet her anger for the moment. She laughed out loud when her brother positioned two slices of mango in his mouth like elephant tusks. For the moment, the pain she'd suffered today was forgotten.

Later that night, Victoria had a difficult time sleeping. She and her brothers and sisters were nestled together in the courtyard, under the summer stars. Victoria heard her mother in the kitchen scraping the *tava* pan and running the water to rinse and clean the bowls from dinner. The kitchen, since it had an open flame oven, was located on a veranda outside the home, and flanked the courtyard. The girl heard her father's boots on the tile as he stepped onto the veranda; she shut her eyes, pretending she was asleep.

Ishaq spoke to his wife in a hushed tone, but loud enough for Victoria to hear. "Oh, our dear Victoria. She has such a loud voice. One day, she will become a voice of her own,"

"Her voice is loud all right," her mother said, scraping the *tava* pan with more vigor than she had before.

"She'd better learn to quiet it down before she gets herself and us into more trouble than she already has. You know what can happen, Ishaq. Some of these cities we move into, people are less tolerant." Her voice rose with emotion. "God only knows what a childlike Victoria could say and then..."

Victoria heard her father gently shush her mother. "God has made her different, so He is going to use her for something different. He is never wrong."

"I pray you are right," she said. Victoria could hear no more of her parents' conversation. Her sister Rozi had rolled over and was snoring gently in Victoria's face. The softness of her breath and the rhythmic, repetitive sounds of her deep breathing lulled Victoria to sleep.

CHAPTER 3

"THE OUTCAST"

Victoria's parents enrolled her in the nearby government school the following year. They hoped and prayed that their unruly daughter would form friendships and learn to calm her anger. They also hoped the school would help protect her from the taunting of the local children.

Victoria looked with anticipation at attending her new school. As she'd learned from moving around so much, new places provided new opportunities. She looked forward to the opportunities she would find at her new school. She wanted to meet other students, to learn with children whose fathers held similar government rank and status as her own. These children would be better suited to her liking and worthy of her friendship, unlike the neighborhood children. There may even be other Christians in this school with whom she could bond.

"Victoria Ishaq," the teacher called.

"I am here," she said, her back straight. Her proud voice permeated the room. Her seat was in the very back of the classroom, so Victoria spoke with extra volume. She wanted everyone to hear her.

Teacher Mahnoor looked up from her roll book, searching for the student whose name she'd just called. Finding Victoria's beaming face from among the other children, her eyes fixed on Victoria's. Immediately, Victoria felt her face flush.

"That sounds like a name for a Queen," Teacher Mahnoor said, her sarcasm thinly veiled. Victoria's hands began to perspire and that old anger began to climb to the surface. "I am like a Queen," Victoria retorted, sticking her chin out – "It was the name given to me at my baptism."

Queen Victoria was a Christian; a girl in Pakistan named "Victoria" would be known to be a Christian. As far as Victoria was concerned, she was proud she shared her name with someone who was a wise leader. She was also proud to be a Christian.

Teacher Mahnoor marched to the jute mat where Victoria sat among the other students. She produced a thin stick the length of a ruler from the folds of her *shalwar*. It was commonly used for pointing to lessons on the chalkboard. Quick as lightning, Teacher Mahnoor rapped Victoria's hand with the stick. Victoria screamed and began to cry.

"Next time, Victoria," Teacher Mahnoor hissed, "you will be more respectful."

Victoria could hear the children whispering around her. They'd witnessed Victoria's punishment. It wasn't the severity of the punishment that had sparked their curiosity; it was because they now knew for sure she was Christian. At recess, no one would go near the proud little girl with the sore hand.

When she asked anyone to play, they ignored her and walked away. It was as if she were less than nothing - worth less than scraps of garbage.

Victoria found a spot away from the others, covered her face with her hands, and began to weep. As much as she tried, Victoria could not stop crying. She could not understand what it was about being a Christian that made other children avoid her.

Finally, able to get herself together, she found herself thirsty. A large clay pitcher containing fresh drinking water sat on a table in the back of the classroom. A glass was attached to the table with a chain. Victoria dipped the glass into the pitcher, filling it with the welcomed water and took a long sip – the same way she had seen the other children drink.

"She drank from the glass! She is *paleed*!" a boy from her class yelled.

Other students joined in the *paleed* chant. Several grouped together and knocked the clay pitcher to the floor, breaking it open with their hard blows. Gallons of water spilled from the pitcher, soaking the jute mats on which the children sat. The books, which she'd placed on the floor next to her mat, were now saturated. Teacher Mahnoor stood idly by in the front of the room until her students had finished destroying the barrel and breaking the glass.

"You should never have touched that glass. It does not belong to you; it is for the Muslim children in this class," Teacher Mahnoor reprimanded the petulant girl. The teacher then made Victoria sit in the back of the classroom, facing the wall, away from everyone else, for the remainder of the afternoon. She was being punished and ostracized for taking a sip of water.

Victoria was considered unclean because of her Christian *zat*. She was not allowed to drink from the same glasses, or eat from the same dishes as Muslim children. As a Christian, Victoria was now an outcast at her school.

At the end of the afternoon when her mother picked her up, Victoria rushed to her, her eyes red and swollen, and buried her face in her mother's *burka*.

"Victoria, what in the world happened?" her mother asked, trying to pull the clinging child from the billows of the *shalwar* pants she wore.

"I'm never coming back here," Victoria screamed, her voice carrying enough that other mothers and children stopped to stare at them.

Victoria's mother knelt, took her daughter's face in her hands and forced her to look her in the eyes. "Why are you acting this way?"

"The teacher is horrible; the children are mean and I'm never coming back here. This is not the place for me."

Susan straightened up with a heavy sigh. "That is enough, Victoria."

Grasping the little girl's hand as tightly as she could, she began to walk. Victoria dug her heels into the ground and continued to scream, pulling back on her mother's hand.

"I will not tell you again. Enough of this," her mother said forcefully, pulling Victoria along as she continued her cacophony of yells and screams.

Their walk home was like a moving thunderstorm; the other mothers stared as Victoria and her mother trudged along the dusty streets until they mercifully came to their home.

Her mother opened the gate to the *ghar*, the house where they lived, and dragged Victoria through the doors and into the great room. She forced her to sit on one of the cushioned chairs.

She removed her *burka* and hung it neatly from a nearby hook then glared at her child sitting in the caned chair, her hair mussed, her eyes swollen and her nose leaking.

"Tell me what happened today," she said, her lips pursed firmly, her eyes stony.

Victoria tripped over her words as she told her mother her tale; how she'd told the teacher her Christian name, how she'd been called *paleed* by the other students, how they'd destroyed the clay pitcher of water after she'd drank from the glass and how the teacher did nothing but watch.

Victoria's mother's eyes became dark with fury.

"You always argue, Victoria. Yes, stand up for yourself when you are feeling persecuted, but do so peacefully. These things that happened today, they are small things. If you keep on like this, I'm afraid greater things might happen to you!"

"Grandfather said our zat is Christian and there's nothing wrong with that. Why can't I tell people that?" Victoria asked, crossing her arms across her chest and kicking her feet.

"Because people in this country don't understand Christianity. They will treat you differently if they know. If they don't know, then they will treat you the same as they do everyone else. It's awful, horrible, but true," her mother said.

"I don't like that," said Victoria, her bottom lip stuck out in defiance.

"I don't either," her mother said, wrapping an arm around her daughter. "That is the world we live in. Maybe one day, all religions, all people will be treated the same and we won't be separated by our differences. For now, we need to do our best to fit in. And you need to do your best at school to fit in."

"I will try mother," Victoria said, inhaling her mother's spicy sandalwood scent, allowing their closeness to comfort her.

Victoria was desperate to make friends, but had strong feelings of being outcast no matter what she did.

She couldn't understand why she was being treated so awfully or what she had done to those children to make them hate her so. She forced herself to remember the words and actions of her grandfather:

"Victoria, you are a voice from God," he'd once told her. "One day, people will look at you for who you are inside, not what color your skin is, what religion you are or what your zat is. They will listen to the words you have to say."

Up to that point, Victoria hadn't understood what her grandfather meant. From this experience at school, his words began to make sense. Except for her religion, she was no different from any other person in that classroom. Each person in that room deserved respect. And Victoria vowed to earn respect from each one of them.

She decided to try again. She would go back to school and make them see her in a different way; she would earn their respect.

Her resolve would be tested with what happened next.

CHAPTER 4

"SHE IS A CHILD, JUST LIKE YOU"

Encouraged by her parents, Victoria returned to her classroom. She was frightened, intimidated and embarrassed, but after recalling her grandfather's great wisdom, Victoria's outlook brightened. This time when her teacher took roll call, Victoria was not disrespectful to Teacher Mahnoor. When Teacher Mahnoor called Victoria by her given name, she merely replied in kind with all the other students. She prided herself on her new self-control.

Victoria took great pains to do everything in the same fashion as the other students; she sat the same way, ate the same way, held her pencil the same way, trained her hair to look like the other girls. She wanted to blend in. By becoming the child the others expected her to be, she would earn the respect she yearned for. At recess, the other children still would not play with the Christian girl and she was always left standing by herself.

One day she decided to take matters into her own hands: she approached two of the girls who had shown her some kindness and asked if she could play with them. They turned their backs and ran to another corner of the playground. After this happened several times, Victoria couldn't hold back her tears anymore. She sat alone in a grassy patch, and cried. She tried to be exactly like everyone else, tried to blend in, but still she was outcast.

Another teacher in the school, Teacher Zubaida, a loving and kind Muslim teacher, approached Victoria. She knelt next to her in the grass. "What's wrong?"

"No one will play with me. I am *paleed!*" Victoria cried, her head in her hands, shoulders shaking from crying so *hard.*

"Why would they think that?" Teacher Zubiada asked, gently rubbing Victoria's back.

Victoria looked up at her. "Because of my *Zat.* My *Zat* is Christian." Teacher Zubaida gave Victoria a hard candy from her pocket and gave her student's hand a squeeze. She stood up and rounded up a handful of girls who were playing nearby.

"This is the only child on the playground who is crying. She thinks you believe she is *paleed.* She is not *paleed.* She's a little girl, just like you, and all she wants are playmates, just like you. Now, play with her."

Victoria smiled at the kindness of the Teacher; she stood up and wiped her tears with the back of her hands. The girls were playing with dolls. While Victoria preferred to play football or kites with the boys, she was not about to let the fact that the girls were playing with dolls derail this opportunity. Victoria sat down with the other girls.

One girl shoved a doll Victoria's way, one they weren't really playing with. Soon after, when the girls noticed Teacher Zubaida was no longer watching, they clustered together, leaving Victoria outside their circle. They whispered to one another so Victoria couldn't hear. Then slowly, they moved away, leaving Victoria with the forgotten doll. Then recess was over.

As the Christian girl grew, she continued to have altercations with Muslim children. When they'd make disparaging remarks about her or her religion, she would hit them or kick them. She had made a choice: she would fight for herself. She lived by the rule, "If someone pushes you, you push back."

Despite the many times her father tried to convince her to not be hostile, Victoria would not listen. She was too angry that the Muslim children chose not to accept her because of her religion.

At those times, she thought of her grandfather and the trials he suffered. Doing that inspired her to fight the same fight that Talib fought. He had chosen to become Christian, embracing the religion even when his life was threatened. She felt that if Grandfather Talib could fight and endure the hardships and social stigmas of being a Christian in a Muslim society, so could she.

Victoria was now too old to have these fits of rage. As she became a young woman she had to learn the ability to control her emotions. Ishaq worried for her and their family. He and his wife, Susan, were afraid there could be an uprising within the community against them.

In the less progressive villages of Pakistan, there had been instances of Muslims taking out their anger on Christians – burning their houses and their churches. Because of Victoria's constant defense of her faith, their family could suffer severe repercussions. Ishaq could lose his job if the community turned against him; they might be beaten, or killed. Victoria could no longer act out so defiantly against her Muslim neighbors and classmates; Ishaq knew something had to be done.

At his wits' end, the anxious father sought the council of his longtime family friend, Colonel Farman. Colonel Farman was Punjabi and a high-ranking officer in the Salvation Army; he was also a well-respected Pastor. He had been a friend of the family for many years; Ishaq referred to him as "uncle" even though he was no family relation.

After dinner, while sipping tea, Ishaq asked to confide in Colonel Farman. In a Pakistani house, a *bethak* is a sitting room that has a separate entrance from the main house, typically reserved for men. In Pakistani culture, a man who is visiting may not walk through the main house and see the wife and children of the man of the house. He is therefore asked to use the *Bethak* entrance, avoiding the interior of the home. The male visitor can then sit with the man of the house, just for conversation, or for any important business. Because Colonel Farman was so venerated and respected, he was welcomed into the family's main house. Wanting some privacy, Ishaq and Susan asked Victoria to go into the *bethak* and read.

After Victoria was out of earshot, Ishaq spoke his mind. "Uncle, I am very worried about Victoria."

"What is your concern?"

"She is a petulant child, Uncle, always fighting any child who speaks against Christianity."

"She has too much pride," Colonial Farman lamented.

Victoria's father closed his eyes and nodded.

"Yes. Being a Christian is something to be thankful for, but too much pride is sinful." Ishaq continued. We both know what it was like being a Christian child in Pakistan. My father was a *Syed*, from a high ranking Muslim family. When he chose to convert to Christianity his own father threatened to kill him."

Uncle Farman nodded. "Being Muslim is more than a religion; it is a set of laws, a lifestyle, a way of being. That would have been a painful decision on the part of your father, one not made easily."

The Salvation Army Colonel set his empty tea cup on the blue, red, yellow and white tile table in front of him. The light evening breeze blew through the archway that surrounded the veranda, bringing with it the many scents of mouthwatering dinners that were being cooked over the open flame ovens throughout the neighborhood.

The frustrated father continued, with tears making tracks down his cheeks.

"I remember the hatred toward me as a child. Because of my dark skin, everyone assumed I was Christian, or Hindu, and I suffered many indignities. I don't want to see the same for Victoria, but she makes it so hard for herself. She simply cannot keep silent."

"Have you considered sending her away to school?" Colonel Farman asked. Ishaq lowered his head, almost shamefully.

"Many times," he said sadly.

"I know there are Christian schools and missionary boarding houses for girls. The nearest one is in Sangla. That might solve some of your concerns."

Ishaq looked at his "uncle" eagerly, hoping he had a real solution for their plight.

"There is a Christian boarding house in Sangla Hill, run by the Presbyterian Church. The school has Christian and Muslim students. There are only Christian students in the Methodist-run boarding house nearby. It is about a half hour journey from here, and she'd have to live there in the dormitories full time. The students in the school are a mix of Muslim and Christian students, but she would go back to a Christian environment after classes ended. Perhaps this would provide enough of a safe place for her, a place where she could concentrate on her schoolwork. If this is successful, you would no longer need to be so concerned."

Ishaq jumped up and shouted, "Uncle, thank you! This is exactly what Victoria needs. She could learn there, thrive and no longer need to be worried about her Christianity. She could make friends with other Christian children."

Ishaq smiled at the possibilities; this was a chance for Victoria to finally find some peace for herself, and for the family, and for him. It was a chance, but no guarantee.

CHAPTER 5
"THE GIFTS OF CHRISTMAS"

I t was Christmas in Pakistan, the Christian children's favorite time of the year. This year, Victoria was given the honor of playing Mary in the Christmas pageant, put on in front of their congregation. A white cloth was put over her head and she donned a simple blue A-line dress. She tucked the baby doll who would be Jesus carefully within her long dress. Normally, Victoria would recoil at the thought of playing with dolls, but not today. Today, it was an honor to hold that small doll because of the grace of what the toy represented: the Christ child.

The Church Victoria and her family attended was in her grandparents' village on the outskirts of Khanewal. This was the village where Victoria had been born. Her grandfather was a high ranking elder within the church, and served members of the congregation through prayer, financial assistance and other needs. People just had to ask, and he would find help.

Their church had been hollowed out from a great mound of mud, accommodated about 100 people, and was always bursting with congregants. There was a bell on top and a simple altar made from scarred, uneven scraps of wood from poplar and mango trees. To Victoria, it was beautiful. The church had no electricity and neither did the small, quaint village where it was located. Men stood in the back of the church pulling strings with shawls attached, trying to keep the air circulating.

Between her grandfather's and father's frequent lessons, Victoria had become fluent in Urdu, and was often asked to read Scripture during worship services. Standing on a bench to reach the makeshift wooden podium, she would read passages from Genesis.

Victoria kept her voice loud and steady as she read. She imagined reaching the congregants who had to sit outside; there was no room inside the mud church. She even imagined reaching some of the townspeople, beyond the walls of the church, hoping they too could hear the power of the words of the Bible.

On this occasion, Victoria tried her best to be reverent as she took her place as Mary, the Virgin Mother. She slowly sat down next to a young Punjabi boy, a new boy she didn't know, who was dressed as Joseph. She looked at him out of the corner of her eye and he smiled back, a wide, toothy grin. Victoria started to giggle, but she held herself in check; she took her role as Mary far too seriously. No child at school smiled at her in such a way. In fact, hardly anyone at the government school looked at Victoria; they did not want to acknowledge the right of a Christian girl to be in their school. The fact that this boy, whom Victoria didn't even know, smiled at her, made her heart leap. That smile was all the Christmas gift she needed.

After church, while her grandfather counted the offerings, Victoria was greeted by many of the church-goers.

"What a beautiful Virgin Mary," one of the elderly ladies from the village said, touching a cold, dry palm to Victoria's cheek. She smiled and thanked the kind woman.

A man and his wife told Victoria how each week they enjoyed coming to church because they were impressed by the way she spoke, and how perfect her Urdu was, and one of her biggest compliments was yet to come.

A lanky teen with a shock of unruly dark hair approached Victoria. As he got closer, he whispered to her, "You did a great job today, Victoria."

Victoria averted her eyes. William was her betrothed, the boy promised to Victoria in the marriage contract between their families. When Victoria turned fourteen, she was supposed to marry the young lad, ten years her senior.

Even though Victoria was only eight years old and didn't understand the concept of love, she did understand that this was the man that she would be bound to in marriage and she took it very seriously. As she considered the boy's compliment, butterflies fluttered through her heart; she dared a peek at this boy who would be her husband. She loved his quirky grin and his soft, kind, brown eyes. She imagined he would be a warm, gentle man just like her father.

"I saw a beautiful flower this morning, and I thought it was pretty, just like you," he said, shuffling his feet.

Victoria drank in his compliments, allowing each one to fill her heart and bring her the happiness intended. All too soon, William's parents had finished expressing their holiday wishes to Victoria's family and other parishioners, and interrupted the conversation between William and Victoria. It was a long journey back to their village and the family was eager to begin their trek. The intended waved goodbye to one another and offered one another shy smiles. Victoria hoped she would see the handsome boy again soon.

She was lost in her thoughts of what her future with William would bring, and jumped when her grandfather, finished with his church duties, came out and took her hand. She felt the rough texture of his hard-working, weather-worn hands, but to her, his touch was gentle. His skin was light, just like hers and she always thought she resembled him. She smelled his scent as he affectionately put his arm around her: his sweat, mixed with juniper. It was a smell that was his alone, an essence that comforted her when she was lonely.

Her kinship with her grandfather went beyond any relationship in her life. She felt they were part of one whole, united in a divine way, something Jesus intended. She looked up, turned her head, and smiled brightly at him.

"I am very proud of you, Victoria," her grandfather said, a small smile on his face. His eyes crinkled at the corners and sparkled with pride. "You are a good Christian girl."

Victoria looked at the ground, her cheeks flushed in a combination of embarrassment and pride. A compliment like that from her grandfather filled her with a joy beyond anyone's understanding. He told her she was a good Christian. In Pakistan that was no easy thing. She promised herself she would remain a good Christian in Pakistan throughout the rest of her life. It was a promise she would not keep.

CHAPTER 6

"SANGLA SCHOOL"

When the new school year began, Victoria found herself in a new school, the Christian school in Sangla. Her father's plan to help his daughter find peace turned out to be a relief, and a challenge.

During the half hour journey from her parents' home to her new boarding school, Victoria chewed her lip until it almost bled. Nervously, she clasped and unclasped her hands in her lap. This was another new beginning; she was starting the fourth grade, middle school.

There was also pain. The grandfather she loved so much had passed away. Victoria had kept much of the emotional struggles hidden. It was at times like these, when a new passage of her life was beginning, that she wished grandfather could be here to guide her. She knew, however, that he would be with her in spirit, and those thoughts helped soothe her grief.

"Victoria, you will love your new school," her father said excitedly as he navigated the dusty, crowded streets of Punjab toward Sangla.

Victoria said nothing in response, the nervous somersaults her stomach was making had kept her mouth closed. While her father continued to comment on how her life would change for the better, her mother remained silent and faced forward, her eyes on the street ahead. Victoria couldn't help but think her mother was happy to be rid of her, despite the caring and careful way she had packed Victoria's belongings. Maybe her mother thought the school would be better able to keep her out of trouble.

Mother and daughter had packed a sturdy metal trunk with all the belongings the girl would need. The boarding house provided little in the way of things that would make her stay seem like home. Her mother packed her uniforms, other play clothing and night garments as well as hair accessories and toiletries, and familiar snacks - dried fruits, almonds and chick peas. These would remind Victoria of home,

Victoria tried to convince herself that this was for the best, but she'd never been away from home for long periods of time before. Never had she slept in a bed that wasn't her own. The thought of not sleeping on the veranda, or in the courtyard with her brothers and sisters, terrified her. The thought of not having her parents nearby if something were to happen made her flinch. As she thought more about it, Victoria could not see how this move to a boarding school would benefit her in any way.

Ishaq and a servant carried Victoria's heavy metal trunk into the dormitory. Victoria and her mother followed behind; the bustle of other children and their families moving into the dormitory surrounded them. There was no sign of Uncle Farman, although her father was sure the Salvation Army Colonel had alerted the school staff to the challenges they would face with their new student.

Arriving young girls greeted one another with squeals of delight and they embraced one another after their long break. Happy chatter and laughter was all around Victoria, but she could find no reason to even smile.

Beds with narrow metal frames and thin mattresses lined the walls in long rows; to the little fourth grader, it looked like an army barracks.

Each child was assigned a closet with a key and keychain which she could wear around her wrist. The closet was where Victoria would keep her personal belongings.

So many young women would live in this one room, each a stranger to Victoria. She fretted that not only did meeting new people hold great potential; it could also hold great misery. She'd learned over time to keep her hopefulness in check; she'd suffered disappointment more often than she'd been surprised with kindness. She could hardly expect this new venture to be any different.

Her mother pulled Victoria's linens from her trunk. With great care, her mother laid her blankets in place, pulling them taut and smoothing them down. In silence, she helped Victoria put her clothing and toiletries neatly into her closet. Victoria looked closely at her mother, expecting to see a frown on her face, a common look her mother wore when Victoria was involved in something with which her mother had to help. She often felt like she could not do anything good enough to please her mother. This time she was surprised to find that her mother's eyes glistened with tears.

Susan looked at her young daughter and swept her up into her arms, hugging her so tightly that Victoria gasped. The love Victoria felt from her mother overwhelmed her and Victoria sobbed into her shoulder. All too soon, her father came between them, and it was time for parents to return to their villages.

"Victoria, we love you and we are doing this because we know it is best for you. For all of us," her father said giving her a tight hug. Her mother wiped her teary face with the back of her hand.

"Papa, please don't leave me here," Victoria whispered, not wanting the other girls to overhear her.

"We must," he said. "We will see you during break. We are not too far away," he insisted. A half hour drive to a fourth grader seemed like an eternity.

"Papa," Victoria cried, a sob catching in her throat.

"Goodbye, Victoria," her mother said, blowing her a kiss.

"Mama, no!" Victoria screamed, chasing after her parents as they left the room. Many other parents were also leaving their daughters behind, but none of their children were as upset as Victoria. None yelled and cried and begged as loudly as Victoria. The other girls began to stare at the new girl, as she was making quite a scene, her protests growing louder as her parents moved further away from her.

A girl with a tight smile silently sat down next to Victoria. When her sobs stopped, the other girl spoke: "My name is Hazel," she said. Her long black hair was pulled back and plaited. Her round face and dark skin were beautiful and radiant. Her eyes shone with delight. Trying to comfort the distressed new girl she began, "I am an eighth-grade student here," she said. "What grade are you in?"

"Fourth," Victoria said, and crossed her arms in front of her. Seated on the edge of her bed, she stuck her lower lip out in protest. Tears still stained her chubby cheeks.

"Are you sad because you will miss your family?" Hazel asked and sat down next to Victoria on the bed. The linens her mother had placed on her bed still smelled of the outdoors of her city, where her mother had cleaned them and dried them in the sun.

"I am sad because this bed is awful. It isn't good enough. It's not what I am used to," Victoria said and lifted her chin into the air, not looking at Hazel.

"I am very sorry the bed isn't up to your standards," Hazel said. "We all have the same bed here. We all learn to accept it. Soon enough, you will find it quite comfortable. You just need to get used to it."

Hazel stood up. In a soft, kind voice she said, "I hope you find peace, sister."

Hazel made her way around the dormitory, speaking to other children, helping anyone who needed it. Victoria remained seated on her bed, her knees tucked up under her chin, her arms wrapped tightly around them. She hoped the scowl she wore on her face would deter any other children from speaking with her.

That night, Victoria cried herself to sleep. While the other children around her slept soundly, Victoria couldn't help but think of her home, her parents and her siblings. How she missed their nighttime noises: the gentle snoring of her brothers, the heavy breathing of her sister, Rozi. She worried that Rozi, who always slept next to Victoria, would not sleep well tonight without Victoria next to her. Nothing sounded right here, nothing smelled right and nothing looked right. It was all wrong, it was nothing like her home. The more she thought of what she was missing at home, the harder she cried.

The next morning the girls' Matron, Alvina, came to wake up the girls and help them prepare for their day. Victoria was impressed with Miss Alvina. While she wore Pakistani clothing, it was pressed crisp and was without a trace of the mud or the dirt Victoria noticed on the hems of other women's *shalwar*. Her hair was twisted into a clean, tight bun. Her shoes, while not new, were clean and presentable. Miss Alvina was a beautifully put together woman. She was a beautiful Christian woman, the type of woman Victoria very much could see herself becoming someday.

The girls rushed around the dormitory, amid morning laughter and chatter, each taking turns in the lavatories, getting washed, taking care of their morning needs, brushing their teeth. Girls slammed their closet doors, put on their uniforms and packed their backpacks for the first day of classes before they went to the cafeteria for breakfast.

The girls were ushered into the cafeteria. Energetic, talking all at once, the girls sat crowded around Victoria on long benches. Food was placed in front of each girl, on a plain, sturdy plate. It was at this moment that Victoria's exuberance for being at the Christian boarding house evaporated.

In front of her was plain pita bread with warm vegetables. This was not a lunch Victoria was accustomed to at home. She would be served *Paratha* bread, a fried bread or *Roti,* the same bread as *Paratha,* but un-fried. Victoria's nose wrinkled in disgust. She would never be given such meager food as this at her home. She crossed her arms in front of her while the children around her ate eagerly, still smiling, still chattering, still happy. Victoria was far from happy.

One of the school matrons, the one who supervised the lunch tables, walked by. She noticed Victoria was not eating.

"Is something wrong with your breakfast?" the matron asked Victoria.

"Yes, this is food for poor people. We are not poor. We never eat food like this at my house," Victoria said, acid in her tone. Her voice was so sharp, it prompted stares from a few of the girls who sat around her, girls who probably were poor and whose breakfast might not have been as nice as this on the average day. Victoria didn't care.

The boarding house in Sangla was free for those families who couldn't afford the monthly stipend. Parents who were better off, who could afford the tuition, paid a monthly sum for room, board and food. Given the Christians' station and class in Pakistan, most of the girls who sat around Victoria had families who could likely not afford the monthly tuition, or the food eaten by rich people.

"Well, this is the food we eat here," the matron said. There was no anger in her voice, no rebuke.

"I am sorry if it's not what you are used to at home, but it is healthy food and it is what we are able to afford so that everyone can eat. We should always be grateful for the food we are given."

The matron walked away, leaving Victoria to stare at her plate, and the other girls to stare at Victoria.

Begrudgingly, she picked up the pita bread, wrapped the vegetables inside and nibbled at the corner. Her stomach began to rebel, showing its impatience with how slowly she was eating. Victoria managed a few more bites of the bland meal, but ultimately could not bring herself to finish.

⊨⊰ ⊱⊨

Outside, each girl stood in line, in uniform, for their morning assembly.

All the teachers took their place in seats on a long, narrow riser, a sort of stage in front of the student body; Muslim day students and Christians from the boarding house alike, all sat together. Four girls took their place next to the teachers on the stage and one child stepped forward.

A girl from her dormitory who was probably in her third year at the boarding school, read from scripture with a slow, careful voice. After the reading, another young girl sang a Christian hymn, one Victoria was familiar with. When she heard other girls around her singing, Victoria opened her mouth and joined in.

A sense of belonging washed over her, as it did each time she was in church. There was a sense of community, bonding, and commitment to their Christian faith. It moved Victoria in a way that she was too young to completely understand; all she knew was that for the first time since setting foot in the boarding school, she was comfortable. She was surrounded by others, children like her, who believed the same things she believed, who knew the same prayers she knew, who knew the same songs she knew. For once Victoria was included. She didn't have to be quiet, didn't have to hide from others that she was Christian, wasn't excluded from what the others were doing around her because of her faith.

After lunch, she and the rest of the students returned to the dormitory to collect their school bags and walk to their classrooms. It would be a few days before Victoria stopped crying herself to sleep at night, and before she could manage to eat a full meal. Unfortunately, that was not the least of her problems.

CHAPTER 7
"THERE ARE CONSEQUENCES FOR YOUR ACTIONS"

After several weeks at Sangla School, Victoria had finally adjusted. The morning routine of waking, washing and attending prayer service followed by breakfast and classes, soon became second nature. She was still unable to make friends as easily as she had hoped. Even among other Christian girls, Victoria found it hard to fit in.

As young as she was, she did not understand that perhaps it was her; maybe she wasn't being much of a friend to others. Being sullen and petulant was not endearing to other children, children who might have been her friends. Her refusal to eat the food that was offered because it was beneath her, and her noisy complaints about the bed not being as fine as the one she had at home, led the other children to consider her spoiled.

Immature, and still angry, and hesitant to meet others because of the rejection she had experienced so often, Victoria responded by making herself emotionally unavailable. Also, she would judge people based on their actions or inactions without considering there might be pain that drives those actions. Victoria's choice was to lash out in anger when someone disagreed with her.

Schooling at Sangla was co-educational until 6th grade, when boys and girls were separated. Many of the Christian girls lived at the boarding house, but others were Day Scholars, students from the local community. Many of the Day Scholars were Muslim students, even though Sangla School was considered a Christian school and all the teachers were Christian.

Victoria had come to appreciate her teachers. These were Christian women, very beautifully dressed and manicured, well-educated and dedicated to educating children. She often imagined herself as a teacher in a Christian school, someone who would be respected, like the women who taught her each day. She wanted nothing greater than to be like them. One of those teachers was Miss Charlotte.

In class, Victoria sat behind a girl who was too tall for her to see her teacher. After a couple of weeks, she grew frustrated at not being able to see Miss Charlotte. The girl's name was Helen. All Victoria could see of the classroom and of her teacher was Helen's back. She could hear Teacher Charlotte's beautiful voice, but not see her. This bothered Victoria more and more with each class. She became more and more angry.

She concluded that the girl who sat in front of her was intentionally preventing her from seeing the teacher.

Instead of speaking to Teacher Charlotte, asking her to move Helen's seat to a better position in the classroom, she acted impulsively.

One day, after Helen got up from her seat, Victoria could see just how different the classroom looked without Helen parked in front of her like a tall building. As Helen began to sit down, Victoria pulled the chair out from under her.

The girl went sprawling onto the floor and smacked the back of her head-on Victoria's desk as she fell. Blood gushed from her wound; Helen screamed.

Shouts of panic rose from the students around Victoria. Teacher Charlotte ran to Helen. "Danai, hurry, get the school nurse," Teacher Charlotte demanded of a student who stood nearby.

Helen was slumped on the floor and sobbing. Teacher Charlotte collected her young student onto her lap, blood still coming from her head.

The school nurse soon rushed into the classroom. After a cursory glance at Helen, she pressed a large piece of gauze to the girl's wound. Both the nurse and Teacher Charlotte helped Helen rise slowly to her feet.

Victoria heard the other students whispering around her. She felt cold eyes boring into her, and realized the other children had seen her hand on the chair that she had snatched from underneath Helen. They knew she had caused the accident. Slowly, Victoria put both hands down in her lap. She prayed the other students would not disclose who had hurt her classmate so badly.

Once the school nurse had removed the bleeding student from Teacher Charlotte's classroom, the students quickly cleaned up the room, rearranged the desks into their former positions and sat down. Victoria was fearful of what would come next, but now she could see Teacher Charlotte clearly at the front of the classroom. There was no one in her way anymore. She had gotten what she wanted, no matter the consequence.

"Students, that was a terrible accident," Teacher Charlotte addressed the class. Her usually soft, sing-songy voice was laced with stress, stress from the chaos that had found its way into her classroom.

One of the boys who sat a row over to the left and a seat behind Victoria, pointed at Victoria and said, "It was her."

Victoria could feel him stare and point at her. She turned around and glared at him. Her moment of happiness was about to be taken from her and it made Victoria furious.

"She pulled the chair from under Helen before she could sit. That's why she fell."

Victoria crossed her arms in front of her and pouted.

"I saw it too," a girl from the back of the classroom added. Soon, several other students spoke up.

Teacher Charlotte quieted the class. They quickly obeyed. Teacher Charlotte approached Victoria's desk.

"Is what your classmates are telling me the truth? Did you do that?"

Victoria's eyes filled with tears. "Yes," she said softly, casting her eyes downward in shame.

"Victoria, what a terrible thing to do to someone! Your classmate is hurt. She is bleeding! She will need to rest in the nurse's office for some time. Jesus always tells us never to hurt one another. Why would you do such a thing?"

The disappointed teacher squatted by Victoria's desk. Miss Charlotte's voice was soft, not admonishing, but her words showed how displeased she was. This upset Victoria to her core. The last thing she wanted was to lose favor with Teacher Charlotte.

"I couldn't see you, Teacher," Victoria cried. Fat tears coursed down her chubby caramel cheeks. "All I could see each day was her back. When she wasn't there anymore, I could finally see you."

Teacher Charlotte sighed. "I understand, but that was no reason to pull her chair out from under her. We could have solved this in a much different way, without anyone getting hurt."

Teacher Charlotte reworked the seating in the classroom. She moved Victoria to the front row, right by her desk. To Victoria, this was the best seat in the classroom. She wasn't pushed back, cast off, thrown to the back of the classroom as she had been in the public school near her family home.

She was no longer stuck in the rear because she was *paleed*. Now she was in the front, the student seated closest to the teacher.

She never understood the teacher was keeping her close to keep an eye on this high spirited new girl. The effect it had on her, however, was positive; it made her more serious about her education.

Her grandfather, Talib, had always stressed the value of education to his children and grandchildren.

"The world is changing, Victoria," Talib told his granddaughter shortly before he passed away. "To be successful in the modern world, you must be educated. Learn as much as you can about as many things as you can."

"I'm going to learn everything," Victoria said with a bright smile from her spot curled on her grandfather's lap.

Talib smiled. "I am the third of nine children. When I was growing up, women were not properly educated. My sisters never went to school," he told her truthfully.

"Why?" Victoria was shocked. The idea of not going to school seemed strange, almost a form of persecution.

"Women were trained to cook, clean and care for the children. It wasn't necessary for them to become educated. Their husbands would earn the wage, so they needed to be educated, not their wives."

"Women were okay with that?".

"They didn't have a choice then, like they do today. Today it is much better for women. They can go to school and earn a wage if they'd like to," Talib said.

"I will earn a wage," Victoria said, determination settling into her cherubic face.

"I am sure you will," Talib chuckled, tussling the thick hair on top of Victoria's head.

"Were you good in school?" Victoria asked. She had been told she was very good in school, that she was a quick, stalwart learner, particularly skillful in language and religious studies.

"Oh yes," Talib nodded. "I was the first person in my village to graduate from middle school. My father was so proud, he sent me to study regularly at the Madrassa."

"A Muslim school?" Victoria asked, incredulous. Her grandfather was Christian. Why would he attend a Muslim school?

"At the time when I went to school, I was a Muslim," he explained. Victoria's mouth gaped open. She hadn't known her grandfather had once been Muslim. It was considered utterly despicable to denounce the Muslim faith, especially to become a Christian.

Abruptly she pushed her grandfather's hands away from her and scowled at him.

"I hate Muslims!" she had said, and climbed from his lap to the floor. She felt as affronted as if her grandfather had slapped her.

"If that's so, do you hate me?"

She remembered considering her grandfather's kind and loving eyes. She couldn't wrap her mind around such a drastic conversion of faith. Because of the problems Victoria had with Muslim students in school, she had grown to have only contempt for Muslims. Now her grandfather had told her that he had been Muslim. How could she hate him? How could someone that she loved so deeply have once been something that she so strongly deplored? Her young mind had trouble reconciling this idea.

"No, I love you more than anyone on this earth!"

Although she meant what she'd told him, Victoria still found herself moving away from her grandfather, as if a level of trust between them had somehow been broken.

"What about my sisters and brothers? Do you hate them?" he asked.

"No, I love them, they are your family. I could never hate them."

"They are Muslims."

Then he told her the whole story. She remembered how she had opened her mouth to speak, but Talib held up a hand to quiet her. She had been sitting on the floor in front of her grandfather, her legs crossed. With her eyes wide, she sat back to hear for the first time a piece of family history she would never forget.

"I became a Hafiz-e-*Quran* at the age of twelve. Do you know what that is?" Talib asked. Victoria shook her head. "It means I memorized the entire *Quran*. That's like memorizing the Bible, word for word, from beginning to end." Victoria's eyes widened in awe and respect.

"I became the most respected Muslim child in our village," he continued. "I was well behaved in the classroom, favored by many students and teachers alike. I became my father's favorite child, the child he put the most faith into. In fact, he recognized my scholarly abilities and went against his nature and encouraged me to learn English. This was the time of the Alligarh movement."

Victoria remained silent. She had read in her history books about the Alligarh movement, but she didn't know what it was. She couldn't fully appreciate the impact it had on her great-grandfather and how it had shifted his thinking against traditional approaches to education.

"The Alligarh movement was a shift in Muslim thinking that drove what has become the modern Muslim educational system. Those who drove it hoped it would create a spirit of progress and opportunity in India during British occupation.

While many Muslims considered the influence of the British to be blasphemous and intrusive, Syed, the leader of the movement, took a different approach.

"Sir Syed Ahmed Khan wanted to create an understanding between the British and the Muslims through mutual education. He saw that the British education system was more advanced in mathematics and science and saw the impact that education would have on the modern world stage and the endless opportunities it could bring to India.

"To bring value to an English education in the minds of the Muslims and encourage their participation was a brilliant idea," Talib said, a wistful look in his eye.

"Education is the most important thing in your life, Victoria. It is the only thing that can make you look at everything objectively. We must acquire knowledge to make an informed decision or opinion. When we don't have proper education and we choose to form an opinion based on limited knowledge or on popular opinion, problems are caused."

"What I am trying to tell you is that you should search things out before you make a decision. You shouldn't get upset about things until you know the whole story. Especially we Christians, we must also learn to forgive the ignorance of others. Often, they do not know what they do."

From that moment, Victoria had vowed to do her best to forgive Muslim children who insulted her with their cruel words. They did not know Victoria, they did not understand her religion. They were not educated enough about her to form an opinion of her. She would try to remember that the next time she was called *paleed* or was insulted in another way. She did her best, until the inevitable next altercation.

Each day in the middle of their studies, students could have a 45-minute recess where they would eat lunch and play, much like American schools. Even at eleven years old, Victoria did not play games that were typical of girls. She much preferred the grittier sports and rough and tumble play of the boys. Victoria's brothers at home always allowed Victoria to play with them while her sisters concentrated on their dolls and Victoria expected the same from the boys in her class. Unlike her brothers, her classmates were far less willing for a girl to interfere with their fun. The most vocal about this was a boy named Sadaqat.

Sadaqat always seemed to pick on Victoria, often for no reason at all.

"Victoria's SOOO rich," he would taunt her. "How come your parents had to send you away to go to school? Wasn't your school good enough?"

Sadaqat was one of the students to quickly point his finger at Victoria when she had caused Helen's accident. He could not waste an opportunity to get Victoria in trouble. When Victoria would ask the boys to play with them, Sadaqat was the first in the group to answer with a resounding *"No!"* and laugh as Victoria walked away saddened.

Sadaqat's father was a counselor at the school, and Victoria thought maybe he felt free to act badly thinking he would suffer few repercussions. It was also possible, however, that Sadaqat was simply an immature young boy, as peevish as Victoria. Whatever the reason, Victoria and Sadaqat got along as poorly as oil and water.

There came a day when, tired of jumping rope with the girls, Victoria decided that today she would join the cricket game the boys were playing. Of course, Sadaqat was playing cricket too.

"Can I join?" Victoria asked.

Sadaqat laughed. "Girls can't play cricket."

"Of course they can," Victoria retorted. "Girls can do anything boys can."

Sadaqat laughed again and a few of the other boys joined in. "No, they can't."

"I will prove it to you then," Victoria said, nodding toward one of the old, splintered, wooden cricket bats one of the boys was holding. She held out her hand to the boy for him to give her the bat.

Sadaqat made a rude, offensive gesture at Victoria. Immediately, Victoria's hands balled into fists. She rushed at Sadaqat and before he had an opportunity to defend himself, Victoria pushed him to the ground. He landed on his back in the hard-packed dirt with a thud, a small sound of surprise escaping him.

Victoria jumped on top of him and pummeled him with her fists. Sadaqat screamed, but she would not let up. She hit him in the face, the arms, the stomach, anywhere she could. His arms flailed, trying to anticipate Victoria's blows as he tried to protect himself. Boys and girls alike gathered around the fighting children. No one stepped in to help; they just watched. Many of the boys began to laugh at Sadaqat.

Soon, Teacher Charlotte and another teacher each grabbed Victoria by an arm and yanked her from her position on top of Sadaqat. She was still spitting mad, her face screwed up in a grimace, her fists still balled. Her eyes were fierce and her face flushed with rage.

A stream of blood ran from Sadaqat's left nostril, his clothing was rumpled and dusty. He wiped his nose with the back of his hand, and as he did, the sight of blood made him howl. Quickly a teacher made her way to Sadaqat's side to console him, and take him to get treated by the school nurse, while a furious Victoria was escorted to the principal's office.

Victoria sat in the principal's office for two periods until her father arrived. His face was stoic; Victoria could not read his emotions at all and this worried her. Usually she could tell his moods, but not today. Another man walked into the principal's office shortly thereafter; Sadaqat's father. The principal had a private conversation with both men for what felt like an eternity. Once the parents emerged from the principal's office, Victoria's father sat next to her on the hard, wooden bench where she had been sitting.

"What happened, Victoria?" he asked quietly. She had enough sense to understand the severity of this situation and respected her father's authority enough to reply truthfully and without sarcasm.

"He told me I wasn't good enough to play cricket because I am a girl!" Victoria began to cry in earnest. She put her face in her hands and her little body racked with sobs. "We are all equal in our house," Victoria cried. "Why not here?"

"You were bullied in public school and it made you angry and upset that other students treated you so badly," her father said, taking her hands from her face so she would look at him. Victoria did so, but felt so guilty she could barely meet his eyes. "Now, you come to this new school, and you become the bully!"

"He said I wasn't good enough!" Victoria exclaimed.

"You and Sadaqat are both Christians. We do not harm others. You will not harm anyone in this way again. Do you understand?" her father asked, his voice low and firm. His dark eyes grew tempestuous as the anger rolled through them like a thunder cloud. He gave Victoria's hands a tight squeeze as if to emphasize his words. "I apologized to his father for you and for your behavior. I pray you will not act this way again."

Victoria nodded. She had nothing more to say. She understood that as a Christian she shouldn't harm another person, but what about when they harm her first? Doesn't a Christian have the right to fight back?

Victoria sighed. She realized that once again she had done something that had been shameful. Her father was a well-respected government officer. He should not have to be ashamed of the actions of his daughter and apologize to another student's parents for her bullish and sophomoric behavior. She should be strong enough to quiet her violent tendencies when she felt provoked. She promised herself she wouldn't embarrass her father ever again.

When Victoria returned to the dormitories, several girls stood around her excitedly, directing questions her way. All day they'd been curious about what Sadaqat had said that had made Victoria so angry. They wanted to know what her punishment had been. They needed to tell her that Sadaqat wouldn't speak for the rest of the day and he had bandages on his head because she had made him bleed.

"I can't believe you beat a boy!" one girl gushed, making Victoria feel like a hero.

"You're so strong!" another girl giggled.

"Tell us what happened," a sixth-grade girl begged.

"Start from the beginning," a fourth-grade girl demanded.

She knew she could never behave that way again, but still, a wave of acceptance by the girls washed over Victoria. She was filled with the warmth of a sudden popularity. For once, Victoria was the star and she took advantage of her opportunity to tell her story from the beginning, embellishing every detail but not straying from the core truth of the story.

"Girls can do anything boys can. Anything!" Victoria finished. Some girls cheered, others smiled, one even reached in to hug her.

At that moment, Teacher Charlotte entered the room. It didn't take her long to find Victoria surrounded by the crowd of curious middle school girls.

Silently, Teacher Charlotte led Victoria to her apartment. She had a small sitting room with two chairs and a table, a shelf on the wall full of books and a small reading lamp. She gestured to Victoria to sit in one chair, while she seated herself in the other. A small window overlooked the courtyard, and a closed door was to Teacher Charlotte's left. This was presumably her sleeping quarters.

Victoria kept her hands clenched in her lap, her eyes downcast.

"What you did today was unacceptable," Teacher Charlotte said.

Victoria's head snapped up. "He was being mean to me," she said indignantly.

"That's no reason to beat him until he bleeds."

Victoria put her head down and her shoulders slumped. She knew her teacher was right.

"You are a beautiful, smart girl. You know girls and boys can do the same things. Boys at your age aren't mature enough to realize that yet. They will, soon enough. In the meantime, don't get involved. Let them make their mean comments, say that girls aren't as good as boys. Let them learn their lesson in their time."

Teacher Charlotte patted Victoria on the shoulder. "No more trouble from you, Victoria." Teacher Charlotte commanded and Victoria nodded.

She made good progress in school, but she was still mischievous, doing things to distract other students. She might throw small stones across the room, distracting students from their work with the clatter it made when it hit the wall. She would build and fly paper airplanes, make fun of students who had bad grades, and dance on top of the desks.

Finally, in a discussion with Teacher Charlotte, one of her teachers said, "Maybe she's behaving this way because she's bored." She was a bright child, maybe she finds her classwork too easy; maybe she needs a greater challenge. The teachers at Sangla School discussed this, and found just the place for Victoria, a place she could not only thrive academically, but remain busy enough so that her idle hands did not do the proverbial devil's work.

Victoria's teachers asked her to help organize the library and clean the chapel. The teachers recognized the girl's respect for both places, and keeping her busy there would help her to keep out of (too much) trouble.

They also realized the deep love she had for her Bible study classes. To involve her more, she was given opportunities to publicly read the Bible; she was hungry to read more of Genesis and The Book of Revelation. When missionaries would come to the school, Victoria would please them with her recitation of Bible passages from both books, and ask them questions, like how Abraham could have thought about sacrificing his son, and why there were the twenty-four thrones in heaven.

There were Bible quizzes and Victoria almost always did well, generally winning one of the prizes. She worked hard to learn as much as she could about the Bible, and took great pride in memorizing as many parts as she could. She thought back to her grandfather, when he became a *Hafiz-e-Quran*, and how proud everyone had been of him. She was about the same age as her grandfather when he received recognition for his memorization of the *Quran*; she wanted to become equally regarded, but for knowledge of the Bible.

She recognized that one of the talents God had given her was the same as one that had been given Talib: she had a gift to be able to read well, and to memorize. Victoria's life at Sangla School changed for the better. It would remain that way, a time of growing and learning, right through graduation, and right up to the time of her upcoming marriage to William.

At fourteen, about to graduate and marry William, she had so much to look forward to. She and William would have a marriage of mutual respect. They could be closer than most married couples, and grow in their faith together.

At this point, she could not have known about an unexpected blow, one that would leave Victoria's family disgraced, and her future in jeopardy.

CHAPTER 8
"DISGRACE"

Victoria was at home after graduation from Middle School. Out in the courtyard of her home, she could hear the angry commotion coming from the *bethak*. Cries of disgust and unkind words spoken in haughty tones; the words cut like razors through Victoria's otherwise quiet home. She'd heard her name spoken, and she heard her father's usually cordial manner take on a sharp tone of indignation.

Victoria's mother scurried about the kitchen, wringing her hands. She seemed to be in search of something to do to keep herself busy and avoid thinking of the conversation in the *bethak*. William's father had come to their home presumably to discuss the marriage between his son and Victoria, but the unkind voices were upsetting the entire household.

As was the custom in Pakistan, families strove to ensure the best possible marriage for their children, and arranged those marriages as soon as possible. Once a marriage was arranged, it was a bound contract and was to be executed as soon as the bride was of age. At age fourteen, Victoria's marriage to William was to take place in short order, but from what Victoria had overheard from the *bethak*, it sounded as if her betrothal was in serious jeopardy.

"What's happening, Mama?" Victoria asked, her voice small. She felt as if she were going to be in trouble, punished for something that she hadn't done.

"Hush! Go back into the courtyard," her mother demanded, her temper flaring. "This cannot be happening," she muttered under her breath as she continued to pace the kitchen floor.

Victoria scrambled to the back door and ran into the courtyard as far away from the poisoned atmosphere as possible.

She sat in a corner of the gated courtyard under a white mulberry tree. Its bony canopy drooped over her, but could not shield her from the disaster that was taking place inside her home. She caught the angry stare of one of her sisters who quickly turned her back when Victoria noticed her. Unable to contain herself, Victoria confronted her.

"What is your problem, Alice," Victoria demanded, her fists locked on her hips.

Alice tossed her long black hair over her shoulder with a shake of her head. "You always ruin everything."

"What are you talking about? What have I done that's upset you this time?"

"Your marriage to William isn't going to happen. Because of that, my marriage options and Rozi's are compromised."

"My marriage to William will happen. You need not worry about that."

"Tell that to father once he tells William's father to get out."

"William's father is here?" Victoria's eyes widened in surprise. She had not expected that her betrothed's father would come to her home. She was disappointed that she knew nothing of it. She wanted to see William. She would convince him that she was worthy of marrying him; all he had to do was come and speak with her.

Alice snorted in disgust. "You head is always in the clouds, Victoria. No wonder William doesn't want to marry you."

"How dare you?" Victoria's hands balled into fists. She was prepared to pummel her sister just as she had that nasty boy at Sangla School.

"Victoria!" her mother screamed from the kitchen.

She narrowed her eyes at her sister in a glare then walked toward her mother.

"Get in here," her mother admonished. She grabbed Victoria by the arm, and ushered her into the main room. Victoria noticed her mother's eyes were puffy and red from crying.

Her father was seated in his chair, his glasses off and resting on his knee. Great lines were etched along his brow. "Papa?" Victoria asked tentatively.

Her father let out a great sigh. To Victoria it looked as if her father had suddenly aged ten years. "My daughter, come here." He beckoned for her to take a seat on the floor in front of him. She obliged, but she could hardly hide the tremor in her hands.

"William's father was here today. He had asked for a visit and I allowed it, assuming he had come to discuss a date for your marriage." Ishaq rubbed a hand over his eyes. "Unfortunately, that was not the case. Instead, he came to break the marriage contract. He told me William had become uneasy about marrying a child. He said Victoria is too young to be given in marriage."

Victoria felt as if she'd been punched in the stomach. All the air in the room had suddenly been sucked away and she felt dizzy. She put a hand on her knees, afraid she might faint.

William? He had rejected her? How could this be? Victoria had thought they were compatible. He always paid special attention to her when she was among the other village children who rushed to his side clamoring for the treats he always seemed to have hidden in his pockets.

Victoria had felt their marriage promise was strong, she knew that she would easily fall in love with William once they were wedded; her feelings toward him were already loyal. What could she have possibly done to cause him to break the marriage contract?

William's father, Robert, and Victoria's mother had grown up in the same village, and had been family friends. When Victoria's mother was pregnant with her, she had told Robert that she wished their families could unite through a marriage. When Victoria was born, a formal contract was made between the two families; William was nine years old at the time. When Victoria turned fourteen, it was time for the marriage contract to be fulfilled.

Victoria turned to look at her mother who was weeping openly, her hands covering her face as she sobbed. "It's my fault. I feel as if I've failed," her mother wailed.

"What happened? Why won't William marry me?" Victoria asked.

The dissolution of a marriage contract in Pakistan is the equivalent of getting a divorce. After that, the woman is considered "damaged goods," and another man is reluctant to marry her. Only if he needs her to mother his children or take care of his home will he even consider taking for wife someone whose fiancé has rejected her.

When word got around that Victoria had been shunned in such a way, her family would be dishonored, and any marriage contract her sisters had would be in jeopardy. People would wonder what was wrong with Victoria that made her so undesirable and they would then assume that Ishaq's other daughters were equally unfit to marry. This was a disgrace the whole family had to share.

"William said that he won't marry a child." Ishaq ran a hand down the length of his face.

Victoria's heart stopped cold. She wasn't a child, she was a woman. She was fourteen, the proper age for marriage. Victoria started to think about her actions; beating that boy at Sangla School, some of the impetuous acts she'd gotten in trouble for; throwing pencils about the classroom, standing on desks and singing. Had William heard about her antics? Did he feel that she was too child-like to support a household because of the things that she'd done? Would he dare to deny their marriage for that?

"We can avoid making anything official. Robert agreed that we would be circumspect about it, saying that we wanted Victoria to go to high school before marrying. It seems reasonable enough, though it might still raise some questions. At least it won't compromise Rozi's or Alice's prospects for the next two years." Ishaq sighed again.

Victoria reached to put an arm around her mother, who was still weeping bitterly. She forced her daughter's arm away. The tears that Victoria had been able hold back this long flowed freely now. She felt that she had gravely disappointed her mother, but she didn't understand what she had done or how she could make it up to her.

Victoria was again at a loss in her life. Again, she was rejected, this time to a point where her whole family had become disgraced. Moving forward, Victoria would have to rely on the charity of some other man to secure a marriage - all because William thought she was too much of a child. She wished she would have the opportunity to talk to him; she knew she could have convinced him that this wasn't the answer to their problem. Victoria could change. She *would* change, for him, for their future.

"I will ask Col. Farman to help us to enroll you in the Salvation Army boarding house in Lahore, and we will admit you to Lucie Harrison Girls High School," Ishaq said. "It's a bit late to enroll, but perhaps there can be some exceptions made."

"Thank you, father," Victoria said softly through her tears, not knowing what else to say. She went through the days and the weeks ahead numb, and in a state of disbelief. Guilt overwhelmed her when she saw the hollowness in her mother's eyes, swollen and red from her constant bouts of crying.

It wasn't until Victoria heard that she was accepted to high school that her mother seemed to fare a bit better. A new, unplanned chapter of Victoria's life was ready to begin.

CHAPTER 9
"A NEW OPPORTUNITY"

I t was time to begin high school. Victoria's mother gave her a soft smile from the front seat of the small sedan they drove through the clustered and congested streets of Lahore.

"Here we are," her father commented, a level of excitement lacing his voice. It wasn't often their family would come to Lahore, so each time they visited the big city, it was a treat. Lahore was the most modern city in Pakistan and was often called the "learning seat" of the country.

Most of the country's premiere schools and universities were housed in Lahore, and only the most exceptional students attended them. With a more gracious outlook toward people of different religions, the boarding house in Lahore, where Victoria would be living, promised her a reprieve. She could be sheltered from the ignorance and prejudices that arose from the people in the more rural communities where she had lived.

The Badshahi Mosque loomed over their family car. In the early morning sun, the orange tint of the mosque became brighter, more stately and commanding. They could see the tall pillars rising into the sky, like grand sentries standing guard. A wide courtyard was spread across the front of the mosque, with an opulent fountain standing as its centerpiece.

Victoria watched as crowds of people meandered through the paved streets; some selling their wares from brightly colored carts, others lounging in the outdoor seating provided by local restaurants, still others shopping. The hum and din of the cars creeping past the crowds of people, the occasional shout of someone being taken advantage of, the bark of someone else's laughter, the scent of mouth-watering cuisine – all these tempted Victoria with the promise of the new perspective eighth grade would give her.

Colorful buses, cartoonish with the amount of gaudy adornments caught Victoria's eye. Brightly colored hoods, skirts that wrapped around the bottom of the car made with brightly colored threads and beads, made her smile. She noticed street lamps that at night would glow like candles and cast soft light on the buildings that lined the streets.

At night, the buildings would look very plain but during the day you could see the beautiful carvings, the balconies built with carved woodwork. The city is one of a kind, with a mix of old Mughal styled buildings, and modern European architecture.

Each building wore a different face; each a different height, width, color and shape. There was no homogenization among these buildings, nothing common except for the fact that they were painstakingly built with great love and care. Victoria couldn't help but think God must have felt the same way when he created man, making each soul different shapes, sizes, colors but each one the same inside, each one created with an equal amount of love.

"This is a real opportunity, Victoria," her father said, their car at almost a complete stop as he tried to navigate through a particularly dense crowd of people. "We should be grateful to your teachers. They saw you had potential and recommended you for high school."

In Punjabi culture at the time, most girls did not go on to high school. High school was eighth through tenth grade. If a girl completed her high school curriculum, she was considered bright

enough to become a nurse or a teacher. Victoria was a quick learner, so sending her to high school had been an easy decision for her
parents and teachers.

"I will miss you," Victoria told her parents.

"We will miss you also," Victoria's mother said.

Victoria noted the sadness in her eyes. The daughter knew she
had been a difficult child, and had caused her mother much du-
ress, especially because of the news of her broken engagement to
William. Their journey had not been easy together, but as Victoria
became more mature, she had begun to concentrate more on her
studies, and her acrimony had dissipated.

"It's such a long drive," she commented, a hint of sadness in her
voice, matching that in her mother's eye. It took two hours to drive
between Shahkot, where her family was living, and Lahore.

"We will see you for Christmas break," her father smiled, ac-
celerating the car so quickly that Victoria was flung back in her
seat. There had been a break in foot traffic so her father had taken
advantage of the opportunity. Still, a dark-skinned man in a cream
colored *kameez* raised his fist and yelled as Victoria and her family
scooted past.

"And Easter," her mother pointed out. "And summer is a nice
break."

"Two months," Victoria murmured to no one in particular.
After seeing this vibrant city, with all that there was to learn in
Lahore, she wondered if the two months she'd have to spend in
her sleepy old suburb would drag by.

They arrived at the school and said their goodbyes. Victoria
walked alone into the dormitory with her belongings. Excitement
coursed through her. There were fewer girls per room, giving her
more privacy than she'd had in lower grades. She had her own desk
and chair; the quality of the craftsmanship impressed Victoria.
The beds were more plush, her assigned area was larger. Victoria
quickly made her bed and flopped down on it.

She had mixed feelings. Instead of getting married and moving on with that chapter of her life, she was going to high school. Once her marriage had been arranged, she never thought she would have the opportunity. Now she did.

Despite the disgrace of William's rejection, she couldn't help but feel grateful. Something she hadn't realized she had wanted was now a reality. She smiled to herself. Victoria had a better feeling about Lucie Harrison High School.

CHAPTER 10
"AN UNEXPECTED ACCEPTANCE"

E ach morning the girls would line up in a ruler straight row and walk the several blocks to Lucie Harrison High School. In accordance with Pakistani custom, this high school provided a single sex education. Victoria preferred studying exclusively with young women; she believed the distraction of boys and their childish antics did nothing to encourage good learning habits.

Lucie Harrison High School was built by an Episcopal missionary from Massachusetts in the 1930's. Only Christian teachers were employed by the school, except for one: the Islamic studies teacher. She was Muslim. Although the school was built by a Christian, the education laws of Pakistan still held true. Any female student who qualified could attend Lucie Harrison High School, even Muslim girls. Students whose families lived in Lahore and who were not in a dormitory, were the Lucie Harrison "Day Scholars."

The Muslim Day Scholars of Lucie Harrison were required to go to Bible study and participate in prayer during chapel. Since Bible study was a part of the curriculum, they needed to attend to pass into the next grade. Many Muslim students willingly elected to take Bible study. This impressed Victoria. She hadn't thought that a Muslim student would want to learn about Christianity, especially since many Muslims that she'd encountered throughout her life regarded Christians with contempt.

As she got to know the Muslim girls, and meet their families, she realized what her grandfather, Talib, had done when he converted from Islam to Christianity. He wasn't just leaving a religion, he was entering a whole new life. It was important to him that his family, especially the youngest, know why he had broken with his family, and his former god.

═╬ ╬═

No one was more intrigued by Talib's past than young Victoria. One late afternoon, when the sun was setting and the heat was waning, Talib sat with his granddaughter and opened more of his past.

He told her about his father, who was a *hakim*, a specialist in herbal medicine; he was considered a doctor. He and his family had lived in a beautiful home in a wealthy part of town and could provide all their children with the best education offered. His father was also a teacher of the *Quran*, and therefore was very influential within his community.

In Talib's younger days, during the British Raj, India was one country with two major religions – Hinduism and Islam. A friend of Talib's, a Muslim named Ahmed, saw the world twisting and changing.

"You must learn English, Talib." My friend said to me. "Your children too. Trust me, my friend, it will become important."

When everyone began to talk about Partition, saying Pakistan and India would become separate countries, Talib knew his friend was right. Anyone hoping to succeed in the modern world would need a good education. At the time, the best schools were the English schools.

He told his granddaughter that he did not feel satisfied with his life at that time. He knew there was something more for him, but he didn't know what. Young men are eager to do bold things. In 1942 he shocked his family when he joined the British military.

He told how this move to join the infidels was a slap in the face to his father. The British were not accepted in noble Muslim society. They were conquerors, invaders. They had usurped the government from the last Mughal Emperor of India and ended Muslim rule! This caused great animosity between the English and the Muslims; the intense dislike created a wide chasm, almost impossible to bridge.

"What did your father say to you when you told him you'd fight with the British?" his young granddaughter Victoria asked, her eyes wide open.

Talib knew that Victoria would understand the courage it took to go against his father's wishes. He saw the same strength in her.

He placed a gentle hand on his granddaughter's head and frowned.

"He was furious. It pained me, but I knew I had to join. At the time, I didn't know why I was so intent upon joining with the British. Now that I look back, I know why."

"Why?" Victoria's stared up at the grizzled old man.

Talib turned his head, his eyes staring at the crescent moon on the top of a nearby mosque. "Because it was after I joined the British forces that I became a Christian."

"What made you convert?" Victoria asked, and swallowed hard. She knew that Talib had been Muslim and converted to Christianity, but it wasn't often that he spoke of it.

Talib felt that the young girl should have some insight into her family history, and that included the story of his conversion to Christianity.

"I wasn't sure how I knew, but something told me that my life was about to change forever."

"Actually, I was the first from my village to join the British army. Most Muslims had no interest in fighting for the British army, but the Hindus. In one sense I was out of place as a Muslim, but I was of Indian background. I spoke Urdu, so the first assignment they gave me was an order to serve in the medical corps with British men."

The little girl listened; she was restless, but intrigued by this family history.

Talib would read the *Quran* every opportunity he had, trying to reconcile within himself how his religious faith fit into the world around him. The British barracks were grand; full of life, bawdy laughter, ale and too much food. Even though Muslim custom prohibited Talib from engaging in much of it, he was nevertheless intrigued.

Each day, the soldiers around him greeted him with a smile, a clap on the shoulder, and the friendly words, "'Ello Chap."

Soon enough he understood this greeting and returned it. He noticed they would smile even brighter when he returned their greeting. He would join the soldiers around the fire pit at night, sit nearby as they ate, and study their movements and words. Soon, Talib could speak passable English.

Because of his father's reputation as an excellent *hakim*, Talib was upgraded to the Army's medical wing. He was given the role of a medical orderly, where he assisted the field doctors with their work. The field doctor Talib worked with was Major John.

Later, Major John would change Talib's life forever.

That was enough for one day. Susan was calling everyone to come to dinner. The girl and her grandfather went into the house.

CHAPTER 11

"MY BROTHER"

From time to time, Talib would fill in the story of why he left his faith and his family to become a Christian. As Victoria learned, it was not something that happened overnight. It was the most difficult and courageous thing he had ever done.

Talib was not converted to Christianity by what followers of Christ would consider traditional evangelism. Rather, his conversion came through the friendship of a Christian man, someone who touched his life with Christ's love. He knew this was something important he had to teach his precocious granddaughter.

Talib had many questions about religion. As a well-educated young man, he asked his revered father questions about religion, hoping for a scholarly, respectful conversation. His father would shut down the conversation before it even began, berating his son for his lack of faith. He demanded that Talib reread the *Quran* and told him to keep any questions he had to himself. Talib was instructed to take the word of the *Quran* for what it was, and believe, without question.

Talib, however, wanted answers, despite his father's commands. When he was in the army and surrounded by English speaking Christians, Talib vowed to ask his questions again.

"Talib," Major John called to him one afternoon as he stocked the medical tents with gauze pads, suture kits, aspirins.

"Sir?"

"You seem tired my friend, anxious." Major John put a hand on Talib's shoulder to slow him from his task. Talib turned to face the officer. Talib's English had improved considerably; he could now understand almost everything that was said to him by the British troops.

"I am worried (Allah forgive me)" he admitted. "With my duties in the army, I cannot pray on time. I am up early in the morning and late at night to get all of my prayers done."

Major John smiled at Talib. "I appreciate that can be difficult for you. Is there anything I can do to help you?"

"How do you do it?"

"Do what, my friend?"

Talib scratched his head. "Keep up with your prayers? You are busier than I."

"I don't have to be on time with my God, Talib. I can pray wherever I am and whenever I can. My God doesn't keep record of that. All He wants from me is that I remember to pray and that I ask for His assistance when I need it. He's never disappointed me."

Talib thought about this carefully. Was Allah listening only during the times of day that was considered prayer time? Or was he always present? Could he listen at any time?

Often Talib would walk by the military barracks in the Jalandhar Cantonment, the area where he was stationed. In the Punjab area that was India during WW II, it was an important military base used by the British as a staging area for the fighting in Burma. For Talib, the Jalandhar Base was his introduction to British culture.

Talib would pause and listen to the soldiers as they talked to each other. Their loud, brash tones and their barks of infectious laughter always fascinated the Indian man; now, more than ever, he wanted to learn their language.

One afternoon, as he was standing close to the barracks, listening to the Englishmen speak, Major John saw him and came outside.

"Talib," he called, surprised to see the man from the medical corps outside of the barracks.

"I was just leaving, Gora Sahib." (During British occupation, Indians called the white men *'Gora Sahib'* or *'white sir'.*) Talib put his head down to walk away.

"Wait," the officer called. "I wanted to give you something." He handed Talib a thick, leather bound volume, it's cover faded and marred.

"I thought I saw you out here. I have a present I have wanted to give you. You've worked hard to learn to speak and read English. Here is a copy of the book that I live by, the words of my God. If you choose to read it, please let me know if you have any questions." He gave Talib a pat on the back and turned back into the barracks.

After Talib completed his necessary duties for the day, he sat with the unexpected gift. "Holy Bible" read the cover. Talib put the Bible aside.

Late in 1942 Major John and Talib would be stationed in Burma, an area weakly defended by the British; most British forces were fighting the Nazi's in Europe. This left an open opportunity for the Japanese, who were looking to obtain raw materials to further their cause. Burma, ripe with resources including cobalt, rice, and oil, seemed a logical place to attack. Once the Japanese secured enough of a foothold in Burma, an attack was imminent. The medical unit where Major John and Talib served faced a dire situation. The unit was on alert.

Soon the Japanese army lined the border of Burma, twelve to fifteen soldiers deep, stretching several miles wide. After successfully taking Victoria Point, the airfield in Tavoy, and the critical city of Rangoon, the Japanese had momentum, and easily flanked out the Allied Burma Corps. The battle that ensued was horrific.

Incredible courage was seen on both sides; so were the deaths and injuries. Talib and Major John were in the thick of the battle.

"Talib!" Major John called as he put pressure on a deep shoulder wound with both hands. Talib ran to his side, a fresh wad of gauze pads in his outstretched hand. A young British soldier writhed in pain on what passed for a treatment table in the medical field tent. Major John snatched the gauze and applied more pressure, handing the responsibility off to another medical assistant as more soldiers were brought in.

Major John triaged each person carted in, assessed their injuries to determine whose injuries required immediate attention, and whose could wait. He did this in a matter of seconds. He barked orders to other assistants, his voice raised over the cracks of gunfire that surrounded them. Short-range Stokes Mortar rounds burst around the medical tent, shaking the ground like an earthquake.

The British trench mortars were used to shoot small, short-range bombs intended to flush out the enemy. Talib noticed some of the injuries that had come into the tent were the result of the men firing these mortars. If the mortar tube was not properly aligned, the legs of the mortar could give way, causing intense recoil and injury to the soldier manning the weapon. One man screamed in pain as Major John twisted a tourniquet around his left arm, which gushed blood.

Talib rushed through the tent and filled demands for supplies, provided assistance when demanded, ushered soldiers carrying their comrades to an available spot within the field tent for treatment. A young Muslim man was carried in on the back of a British soldier, his left leg gone below the knee. Talib recognized him as a man from the village. He listened as the British soldier spoke to the villager in calm, soothing words, words the villager couldn't understand.

Talib understood, and he translated the words into Punjabi. The fear, heavy in the village man's eyes, dissipated as he listened to the words Talib spoke to him. They were words from Scripture, Isaiah 41:10: "Do not fear, for I am with you; do not be dismayed for I am your God. I will strengthen you, I will help you, yes, I will uphold you with My righteous right hand."

Several mortar rounds fired at once, the blasts so close they rocked the tent. Talib was thrown to the ground as one mortar burst right outside of the tent sending shards of shrapnel into the field hospital. The screams of the wounded filled the air.

"He's down!" a soldier yelled.

From his position on the ground, Talib saw Major John trying to cover a gushing wound to his own neck and shoulder!

Talib didn't think about it, he just moved into action. He tossed the wounded Major over his shoulder and ran. He ran out of the field tent and back toward the barracks, over a mile away. Talib was big; he stood over 6 foot tall. Major John was slight and wiry so putting him over his shoulder wasn't too difficult. The British soldiers covered Talib, prepared to shoot should someone fire on him, as he carried the Major to safety.

Once in the barracks, Talib set Major John on the wooden floor to assess his wounds. By now the British Major was unconscious from shock and blood loss. A thick slice of shrapnel had lodged in Major John's shoulder. Talib yanked out the metal and immediately put pressure on the puncture wound, using his shirt to bind the wound tightly. He hoped he had gotten the entire piece out from the wound.

After the blood flow stopped, Talib still sat by the doctor, checking his vital signs. He stayed and waited for Major John to regain consciousness. Soon, the doctor's eyes fluttered open.

"Talib," he said, giving his assistant a thin smile.

"You'll be ok, Major John. I got it out."

"I'm sure you did, 'old chap. You're a fine doctor."

"I'm no *hakim*," Talib said and averted his eyes.

"You're a damn fine one," Major John said.

Talib hadn't expected that compliment, especially since he'd never had medical training other than what he'd learned in the medical corps.

"You saved my life."

"It was nothing," Talib said. He then realized that wasn't true. It was something, something very important.

Talib was old enough to remember the stories of how the Westerners had invaded India and taken over their lands. He'd always wondered who the British were and why they fought so hard to take away the lands that rightfully belonged to the Indian people. All his life he had seen the hatred and the mistrust that had built between the Indians and the Westerners.

What Talib also knew was that, before the British came, the Persian Muslims had infiltrated India and taken land from the Hindus. Where did the need come from that drove men to so much hatred, so much conflict, so much war? What would it take for people whose religions spoke of peace and respect to practice what they were taught?

Talib was born a high caste Muslim man, someone who wouldn't eat off a plate that a Christian had eaten from. He would not fraternize with Christians – they were impure and unclean; it was beneath his status in the Muslim religion.

Today, Talib's hands were covered with the blood of dying Christian men, men whose lives he was trying to save. The religious *zat*, caste, system Talib had been taught meant nothing in the field hospital where he'd worked. The only thing that mattered was saving lives, no matter if they were Christians, Hindus or Muslims.

In the field hospital, people worked together for the good of the group. They put their prejudices aside, and were bound together through the needs of those who were hurt. This filled Talib with great and unexpected, joy.

"You're welcome, my brother," Talib whispered.

CHAPTER 12
"AN UNEXPECTED INVITATION"

There were other times Victoria would be schooled by her grandfather. Listening to him, she learned that reading the Bible opened his heart to Jesus' words. It was courageous, since the new life he would enter went against all the things he'd been taught. He could not help himself.

⊷⊹⊶

After the terrible experiences he'd had on the battlefield in Burma, Talib was given a leave from the army. He returned to his family home, but brought along the Bible Major John had given him; he read it from cover to cover. Since it was written in English, Talib had little worry that it would stir any concerns among his family members. None of them could read English.

While on leave, he received an invitation from Major John to dine at his quarters. Major John's home was built specifically for a high ranking British military official. It was made from brick, large, austere, and protected behind a huge iron gate. It had an ample courtyard tucked around back of the house. Inside, the rooms were spacious and cool. The brick walls absorbed the heat and a breeze blew gently throughout the home.

It was an honor for a regular Indian man to receive an invitation to the home of a ruling British authority, but it made him nervous. Many Muslim customs might be compromised while dining at the home of a Christian.

Talib struggled with his attire. Did he wear the traditional straight cut, white *shalwar kameez* with the red waistcoat? Or should he wear his Battle Dress uniform from the British Army, the blouse with the pleated pockets and exposed buttons and the pleated tan trousers with the exposed shank button? He opted to wear the Battle Dress uniform, thinking this clothing would be the most appropriate.

Major John greeted Talib joyfully.

"Welcome, my friend!" Major John clapped Talib on the back and ushered him into the dining area where a large feast was set upon the table. He showed Talib to his place at the table, where they joined Major John's wife and three children.

Talib froze. In his family's house they did not use a dining room table or chairs. They would eat sitting on a large white sheet that was spread across the floor. He was uncomfortable, but took the seat offered him next to the officer whom he so much respected.

"I'd like to begin the meal with a prayer," Major John announced. His wife and children clasped their hands together and bowed their heads.

"Dear Lord, we are blessed to have our friend Talib here with us today. He is a man who made great sacrifices to save my life. We are grateful for the food at our table tonight, for the gift of Your bounty, for entrusting us to live as You have asked us to. Please help us to grow in Your grace, bless us with Your kindness and help us to be kind to others, looking to You as our example. For these and all blessings, we give You thanks. Through Jesus Christ, Your Son we pray. Amen."

Talib was shaking. He could not accept any of this food. His Muslim faith would not allow it. How could he eat of this feast after it had been blessed in the name of Jesus Christ, a God he did not serve? It would be a direct affront to Allah.

The Hindu woman who served as cook for Major John's family began to serve dinner and a knot twisted in Talib's stomach. What if she was serving pork? As a Muslim, the consumption of pork is forbidden. Talib politely declined the first course and sipped a cup of water while the others dined.

Talib politely declined the second course as well.

"My friend," Major John asked quietly. "Is everything all right?"

"Yes, sir," Talib said, his eyes cast downward.

"What is bothering you?"

Talib could hold it in no longer. He trusted Major John and knew Major John would never judge him. "I am sorry sir, but I cannot eat the food."

"We can serve you something else, if you prefer," Major John's wife said. Talib met her kind eyes, and then looked down.

"I do not want to offend you, but I cannot eat food that's been blessed in the name of Jesus Christ the Son of God. I do not agree with your religion and it would be immoral for me to eat food blessed on behalf of a God I do not follow."

Talib took a deep breath and continued. "I cannot eat with utensils or upon a table where pork may have been served. That too would be a violation of my religion."

Major John smiled. "We are not offended, Talib. We know it is against your religious beliefs to eat pork, so we did not serve any. We understand that those are tenets of your faith and we respect you and your faith. I've invited you here because I value you and our friendship. The last thing I want is for you to feel uncomfortable in our home."

Talib took a deep breath. Major John understood, as a true friend would. He ate the rice pudding that was served later in the meal.

Talib went home and told his parents and wife about the dinner. He told them how he was unable to eat at Major John's home and feared he may have offended him.

"You must invite the Major here, to our home," his mother insisted. "We must make sure this offense is erased."

Talib sent the invitation off to Major John, certain he would decline. To his delight, Major John accepted. Then he thought of his father and how offended he would be that his son invited a Christian man into his home. What had he done?

CHAPTER 13

"A BRIDGE IS BEGUN"

"Were you excited he was coming to your house?" Victoria asked, her brown eyes wide and eager. As a young child, she loved the idea of having a friend come to her house to see where she lived, meet her family and play with her toys.

Talib frowned as he recalled the meeting between his major and his family. He should have seen and understood then the angry side of his father, the one that confronted him when Talib told him he had become Christian.

"I was excited. I wanted my family to meet this man, this Christian man who had become my friend." Then he went on with the rest of the story.

◆━━◆ ◆━━◆

Talib's mother set the dinner on the *tarkhawan*. Her son was more and more afraid that the Major would be insulted while at his house. After all, the British family had sat around the dining room table in wooden chairs. His fears were unfounded.

As they sat down for the meal his mother had carefully prepared, Major John sat with them on the floor, his legs crossed like

Talib and his father. He gave no indication that he was uncomfortable or offended.

After Talib's mother and his wife had laid out all the food for their meal, Talib's father prayed over the food. Major John remained quiet and respectful. He did not outwardly offer a contradictory Christian prayer, though Talib thought Major John may have given thanks to Jesus silently.

Major John refused no food and tried everything that was offered. Many times throughout the meal, he politely showed his gratitude to Talib's mother and wife for preparing a lovely feast.

As they ate, Talib noticed his father staring at Major John as he sipped his cup of chai tea or scooped some *raita* from the communal bowl. It was not a look of respect, but a look of resentment. In the end, his father said nothing to embarrass them.

After Major John left that evening, his father went immediately into the kitchen where his wife and daughter-in-law were cleaning up.

"You've destroyed the dishes the infidel ate from, didn't you?" he demanded.

Talib's mother nodded and pointed to the scrap bucket where they kept the garbage. Inside were the cup, bowl and plate Major John had used during the meal. With a curt nod, his father left the kitchen and went into the *bethak*. Talib followed him angrily.

"Why did you do that?" Talib asked, unable to suppress his fury.

"I don't know what you're talking about."

"Why did you throw away those dishes?"

"We do not eat from the same plates as the infidels. You know that, Talib."

"Major John is different."

His father sighed. "I don't care how nice he seems. He is a Christian from the West. They are infidels, nothing more, nothing less." His father picked up the newspaper to indicate their conversation was over.

"He has saved the lives of many Muslim men. He doesn't look to see if they're Muslim, Hindu or Christian. He looks at all lives the same, regardless of their religion. I fail to see why you can't do the same."

"With this attitude, you'll soon become Christian yourself." His father snorted. "This war seems to have gotten some false beliefs into your head. You'd better read some passages from the *Quran* and start saving your rupees so you can go to the Haj for forgiveness."

><+ +><

"Was that the last time you saw Major John?" Victoria leaned in closer to her grandfather, her eyes wide, begging him to continue.

"No," Talib said, and a wistful, faraway look crossed over his face. After a long, thoughtful pause, he continued the story.

I started reading the Bible, the one given to me by Major John. The words entered my heart like cool water on parched earth. My life was refreshed. I began to pray to the Lord to give me wisdom. The more I read, the more I knew God's love. The more I felt love for all, even my family, my father.

"You did become Christian," Victoria exclaimed. "Your father was right."

"My father was a wise man, very bright. He was an excellent teacher and an even better Muslim. I wish we could have come to an understanding about our different religious philosophies."

"My new faith was wonderful. I felt a kinship, a brotherhood, with this white man, and all the other men in the army. The villagers too. Muslims, Hindus, everyone. I even sensed the humanity of the Japanese we fought against. It was then I realized that Jesus wanted us to treat each other all the same.

"I understood what Jesus said in my Bible, in 1 John 4:20, 'If someone says "I love God" and hates his brother, he is a liar; for the one who does not love his brother whom he has seen, cannot love God whom he has not seen."

"Not all people are easy to love, grandfather." Victoria thought of the many children and teachers who had rejected and despised her because she was Christian.

"I'm sure even Jesus was challenged to love everyone," Talib said with a smile. "We are, after all, human. We are not perfect. We will fall, we will make mistakes, we will hurt one another sometimes. We must learn to forgive anyone who hurts us. That's what can make a human being special."

"Muslims don't understand us," Victoria pouted.

"Muslims are human beings who love, cry, hurt just like everyone else. Their beliefs about God differ from ours and sometimes we don't understand them either. That's when we have conflict. When people choose not to understand one another, bad feelings find fertile soil in which to grow."

"Like the children at school," Victoria nodded.

"Yes, my child. As you grow, you will move beyond that. I know you will do better. Like me, you will work to create a bridge of understanding between Christians and Muslims and other religions as well."

"I will grandfather!" Victoria grabbed him in a tight embrace. His big arms wrapped around her and soothed her spirit. She loved being so close to him.

CHAPTER 14
"BUILDING THE BRIDGE"

A s she rode to Lahore for her second to last year of high school, Victoria recalled the many conversations she and her grandfather had together. She wasn't sure why she'd spent so much time thinking about him now. Maybe it was because she knew that soon her life would be hers to live. She would have many choices to make about her future, and she valued the wisdom of her grandfather to help her with those decisions.

At Lucie Harrison High School, students could choose to take Islamic studies or Bible studies. Half of the students in Victoria's class were Muslim students. Because her school was traditionally categorized as a Christian school, Muslim students were expected to participate in Chapel time. Each Christian student had a choice of whether to take a course in Pakistan Studies, or, a Civics and Ethics course. Earning successful marks in these courses was required to graduate from high school.

Victoria was encouraged by the number of Muslim students who elected to take Bible studies. She recalled the wise words of her grandfather. He believed no bridge of understanding could be built between Muslims and Christians if they did not work to accept one another. This was best done by educating themselves about each other's beliefs. Victoria saw that the Muslim women who shared her Bible study classes were examples of what her grandfather had meant.

To share in building this bridge of understanding between Muslims and Christians, Victoria elected to take Islamic studies. After all, her grandfather, whom she admired, had once been Muslim, and had never said anything disrespectful about Islam. Further, he still spoke of his own father with pure devotion, even though his father cast him out of his life after converting to Christianity. Talib radiated forgiveness, but even though she tried hard, forgiving the slights of the followers of the Pakistani Muslims was difficult for her.

It was even harder for her parents to understand their temperamental daughter.

"Victoria, what brought about your change of heart?" her father asked as he signed the papers to allow her to shift her course of study from Ethics, which many other Christian students were taking, to Islamic studies.

"You seem surprised, father," Victoria smiled.

"I am," he replied with a chuckle. "The teacher must have told you that Islam believes in the Bible and in Jesus."

"Grandfather told me that," Victoria admitted. "He was once Muslim. I want to become educated about it. I want to see for myself the differences between the Bible and the *Quran* and their teachings. I no longer want to pass judgment. I will seek understanding through education."

"You sound just like your grandfather." Ishaq handed Victoria back the paperwork, his signature approving her requested change scrawled at the bottom of the form. "I look forward to learning from you."

Victoria couldn't stop the smile that spread across her face.

Back at school, as she put her belongings into the closet that would be hers in ninth grade, she thought of something else her grandfather would remind his children and grandchildren: "When someone asks you what your zat is, you tell them, 'There is no zat system for human beings, only for cats and dogs!'"

This phrase had made her and her siblings roar with laughter, and they'd pretend to crawl about the floor as animals, barking and mewling.

Now, as a young woman, her grandfather's words meant much more to her. They reminded Victoria that she was more than her family name or her religion. She was her own, unique voice and spirit, which transcended any label or any stereotype or judgment that her culture placed on her.

As Victoria began her new courses, she found Islamic studies of great interest. She learned rapidly, and absorbed the teachings of the *Quran* as quickly as she had those of the Bible. In fact, her marks were better than those of most of the Muslim students in her class. Victoria read Arabic with ease, and often her teachers asked her to recite verses from the *Quran* in front of the class. Victoria wondered what Talib's father, her great-grandfather, would have thought of a Christian girl who was proficient reciting passages from the *Quran*.

One afternoon in her Islamic Studies class, Victoria almost jumped out of her seat. The teacher was saying that it was blasphemy to call Jesus "the Son of God." Her eyes narrow, and her hand shot up. The Muslim woman teacher, whom Victoria greatly respected, called upon her.

"Why is Jesus not called the Son of God in Islam? The Bible calls Him the Son of God, and you said a Muslim's faith cannot be complete without acceptance of all four books: the Torah, the Psalms, and the Bible. The Bible says Jesus was the Son of God. How can you say He was not?"

"Because that is what the *Quran* says."

"That doesn't make any sense. If one of the holy books says Jesus is the Son of God, how can you claim He is not?"

This granddaughter of Talib felt herself flush with anger. Immediately, she reminded herself that, as a young woman, she needed to diffuse those feelings, and not act upon them.

Her teacher stopped and stared at Victoria with piercing eyes; the teacher's mouth was drawn in a straight line. In a quiet, but commanding voice, she said, "In Islam, we believe what the *Quran* tells us, exactly as it is written. Any question of that tenet is not only blasphemous, but insulting."

Victoria started to blurt out that it was even more insulting to not answer someone's questions of faith. Then she thought better of it, and said nothing more.

When Victoria returned to the dormitory that evening, she began to write poetry, sometimes in Punjabi, sometimes in English. In her poetry, she shared her frustration trying to reconcile the differences between Christianity and Islam. She found this to be therapeutic. It helped to keep at bay emotions which might otherwise become uncontrollable.

During her ninth-grade year, Victoria experienced a time in life when she was at peace with herself. She was finally able to feel comfortable in her own skin. She had friends, other Christian girls like herself, who believed the same things, thought the same way and enjoyed the same things she did.

She had teachers, Muslim and Christian alike, who recognized her insatiable curiosity. With the help of her Christian and Islamic studies, she developed a mind that could handle deep theological questions; now she believed she could find the answers she needed. In 1977, everything changed in Pakistan.

CHAPTER 15

"NATIONALIZATION"

I n the middle of 1977, the Prime Minister of Pakistan, Zulfikar Ali Bhutto, was deposed in a military coup. The coup was led by Islamic political parties headed by the Chief of Staff of the Army he had appointed, Muhammad Zia-ul-Haq. The *Jamat E Islami* was the oldest and most progressive party that spearheaded this movement. Zia rebelled, and after a period of civil disorder, Zia ul-Haq took over, imprisoned Bhutto, and declared martial law.

To this day, Zia remains a polarizing figure in Pakistani history. On one hand, he is credited for the prevention of widespread Soviet occupation in the region. He also bolstered ties with China and the West that contributed to great economic prosperity. On the other hand, under Zia's rule, Pakistan's relations with neighboring India turned sour. Worse, Zia introduced laws that encouraged great religious intolerance. As a young Pakistani Christian woman, Victoria was greatly affected by the laws passed under Zia's rule.

Zia's rule started with martial law, instituted while Victoria was on summer break. All summer long she heard her parents talking in hushed voices about the Christian institutions that were absorbed by the new regime. Christian schools across the nation were nationalized and Christian students were forced to learn Islamic studies. Private education was no longer available for them.

The new government nationalized all Christian hospitals. Additionally, all Pakistani residents were issued government ID's which identified their religion.

One morning, in a sullen mood, Victoria was at home eating breakfast. She was frightened of what her final year of high school might be like. One thing was sure, it would be very different from the Christian school she had known and loved. She lived in fear of what she might find when she returned in a mere couple of weeks.

As Victoria picked at her breakfast, Ishaq, her father, walked through the house preparing to go to work. He no longer wore the smart suit she was used to seeing him in. Instead, he now had to wear the traditional garb of a Muslim man, an *Awami* suit; traditional *shalwar* pants paired with a long shirt that draped almost to his knees called a *kameez*.

"What are you wearing?" Victoria snapped, surprised, and a bit angry.

"Young lady," her mother, Susan, hissed. "Do not disrespect your father like that."

Ishaq put up a hand to hush the two women. "This has become mandatory dress for all professionals."

"That's unacceptable. You are not a Muslim, you need not dress like one." Victoria's anger flared beyond her control. She could no longer stifle it.

"It is a cultural shift, nothing more. We are asked to free ourselves from the oppression of Western wear and return to our traditional roots."

"Never." Victoria slammed her bowl to the floor.

"Victoria," her father bellowed, his voice raised like she'd never heard before. "You will become more understanding and you will accept the Pakistani culture. You have no choice. Please, accept it and do NOT question it. More hangs in the balance than what you realize."

"You are old enough to accept what your father has said and understand that he has good reason to say it. You will listen." Her mother swept Victoria's half eaten breakfast bowl from the floor and stormed into the kitchen.

"Victoria," her father sat in front of her took her hands in his. "As Christians in this country, things have become very dangerous for us. Please, let it go. Please. Otherwise, you could be killed and so could I or your mother, your siblings..."

Her father's eyes were filled with fear. "I can't talk about what could happen anymore, but please, for the sake of all of us, be quiet. Don't say anything that could inflame anyone."

Victoria stewed over her father's words all day long. She did not want to believe that Christians were now in a position where they could be killed simply for believing something different. It was unfair, it was wrong, and sinful. Along with Victoria's growing anger came that all too familiar feeling of persecution and the cold fear that accompanied it.

All too soon, Victoria's summer vacation ended and she returned to Lahore. She hoped that not too much had changed, since Lahore was the educational seat of all of Pakistan and its liberal epicenter. When she arrived, her worst fears for transitioning back into the same school she'd left a few scant months ago, were realized.

Large walls had been constructed separating her boarding house from the adjacent school. While the boarding homes remained independent under the laws passed by the new regime, all schools and colleges had become the property of the new government.

The tone of the boarding house had changed entirely. The cacophony of excited voices, the sounds of closets slamming and the snapping of fresh linens as they were placed over new beds, were subdued. Students, both new and old, spoke to one another only in hushed tones. Everyone put away their belongings quietly, almost as if they wanted to be invisible or disappear from the insurgents who had taken over their country.

The attitude of the girls in the boarding house echoed her father's words to her: 'Be quiet, accept, understand.'

Suddenly, the girl who had become comfortable with herself, her Christianity, and her place in the world, was once again silenced because she was a Christian, because she was different.

As the young women gathered for the morning assembly, which had once been the recitation of a Bible verse, followed by spiritual hymns, a woman Victoria had never seen before stood before them. She read a passage from the *Quran*, and after this, the students and faculty sang the Pakistani national anthem, indicating the close of the morning assembly.

During the assembly, Victoria, now in shock, looked around her. The Christian teachers stood still and stoic as the *Quran* was read. They dutifully sang the words to the Pakistani national anthem:

"This flag of the Crescent and the Star, Leads the way to progress and perfection, Interpreter of our past, glory of our present, Inspiration of our future, Symbol of Almighty's protection."

The Students of Lucie Harrison School sang the words, but most were singing without the fervor with which they would have sung the Christian hymns.

Victoria became indignant, angry, and fearful. Why were these devout Christian women unable to stand up for themselves, for their religion, for their faith?

The new government strongly favored Muslims, and Victoria saw that many of the Muslim students, whose class, or zat, had been elevated, had become haughtier in their treatment of their Christian classmates.

Victoria took great care to control her rising anger during these changes. Her Christian teachers helped with this by not allowing the students to feel the political pressure from outside. They said nothing negative about Islam, or those who practiced it. They successfully kept politics out of the school and taught their lessons without prejudice. This example helped keep Victoria's anger from growing so strongly within her that she could not control it.

As Victoria's first year of high school wore on, her success in Islamic studies elevated her in the eyes of her teachers. Even the Muslim teachers began to favor Victoria.

One afternoon, Victoria was called to the principal's office. Mrs. Peters, a Christian woman, had retained her role as principal, despite the political shift of the school.

"Victoria, you've been voted the best student at Lucie Harrison." The student covered her mouth with her hand, trying to hide her gasp of surprise. "Thank you," she finally managed.

"You've received the highest marks in Islamic studies. This is an impressive accomplishment."

She'd worked hard, certainly, but had not expected this.

"We would like to ask you to be Head Girl here at Lucie Harrison High School. In that role, you will conduct the morning news and announcements. How does that sound to you?"

A grin broke out on Mrs. Peters face. Her plain countenance lit up with the beauty of her bright smile and Victoria couldn't help but smile in return.

"Then I can begin my announcements with Christian prayer."

Mrs. Peters smile faded. "I'm afraid not, Victoria."

"I don't understand. As Head Girl I am given permission to address the school population. Why can I not do so with prayer?"

Mrs. Peters looked around her as if to see if anyone were listening. She put her elbows on her desk and leaned in close to Victoria.

She looked her directly in the eye and with her voice hushed she said, "Please, Victoria. I know this is difficult and it's a big change. Since we are no longer a Christian school and are now considered a public school, we can no longer pray."

"But there is Muslim prayer," Victoria objected.

"For now, that is the law of the land. We must accept that." Mrs. Peters sat back in her seat indicating this line of conversation was over.

"Congratulations on your achievement."

Victoria opened her mouth to argue with Mrs. Peters, to condemn the law, to protest that the law was unjust. Instead, she remembered the respect her Christian teachers had taught her, and nodded her acceptance of the rule.

"Thank you," Mrs. Peters said, understanding that Victoria's nod meant much more than an acknowledgment of her achievement.

A knowing look passed between the two Christian women and Victoria promised herself she'd remain silent until there was no potential for government backlash.

At that moment, neither Mrs. Peters nor Victoria had any idea that they would be witnesses to how dangerous it had become to be a Christian in Pakistan.

CHAPTER 16
"THE PROTESTS BEGIN"

V ictoria's mother and brother traveled by bus to Lahore to pick her up from school for spring break. When they arrived, Victoria's brother was asked to wait outside. It was inappropriate for a young man of his age to be in the private living quarters of young women. He waited at the boarding house gate while his mother entered to retrieve her daughter.

Inside, many girls milled about with their families and collected a few things for the two-week holiday to celebrate Christ's resurrection. While Victoria waited for her family, she made careful choices of what she would bring home. Soon, she noticed her mother in the doorway.

Victoria's mother stood waiting in her *burqa,* covered from head to toe. It was a look Victoria would never get used to. Her mother was so beautiful, her features delicate and soft. The *burqa* covered her delicate nose, her dainty chin and her warm, comforting smile. There was something else about her mother that wasn't quite right. It was the way her mother stood, her back rod-straight. She twisted her hands together, something she only did when she was nervous.

"Mother?"

"Please Victoria, right away, gather your belongings."

"I'm almost finished."

"Make it fast."

"Is the bus leaving soon?"

Her mother's eyes flashed with fear and she bit her bottom lip. Victoria knew her mother did not want to tell her the truth, so she scrambled to finish packing.

"There is unrest in Lahore. People are protesting Bhutto's imprisonment. I'd like to get on the bus and head back to Shahkot before it gets out of hand."

"What kind of protests?"

"They are protesting Bhutto's execution.

"I don't think they would try to hurt us."

"I wouldn't be so sure, Victoria. Things have changed for all of us, and this is a time of much doubt. No one can predict what might happen; nothing like this has occurred in Pakistan before."

"I understand, mother," Victoria said.

She quickly stuffed one or two last things into her valise and snapped it shut. Victoria's mother closed her eyes and breathed a sigh of relief. The two women picked their way through the lingering students and their families, making their way quickly to where the bus was parked.

Victoria and her mother boarded and took their seats alongside Victoria's brother. The humidity had risen quickly and the air felt dense, viscous. She peered through the open bus window and witnessed an uncomfortable sight.

Lahore's residents were on edge. People pushed past others with angry shouts; profanity shot through the din. To Victoria, even the sounds of the car engines seemed aggressive. Stray dogs slunk away into alleys, tails tucked between their legs. Street vendors were hurriedly packing in their wares. A tempest was swelling along the streets of Lahore, unforgiving of anything in its path, including the bus they were on.

From among the crowd packed together on the dusty road-ways, a horde of people swirled around the bus, in what seemed to Victoria a dance of discord. Shouts grew louder, horns blared and the bus rocked from side to side as masses of people collected around it and began pushing the bus.

Victoria clung to her mother in fear as the mob of angry men pounded on the side of their vehicle, shouting insults through the open windows. Victoria's mother pushed her aside and snapped the window shut despite the heavy humidity. In response, a member of the mob gave her mother a rude gesture which caused Victoria to gasp.

An instant later, a high-pitched scream pierced through the cacophony of the surging mob. Then an acrid stink assaulted Victoria's nose and with it, the sight of smoke. The cries of the mob grew louder, rising to a new level of anger.

"My God," Victoria's mother whispered and she drew her daughter closer to her. Victoria turned her head as far as she could and saw that something was on fire. Flames licked the air, smoke billowed and the crowd pulled back to give the conflagration a wide berth.

"Is that a man? On fire?" Victoria asked.

Whispers turned to murmurs turned to shouts on the bus as people realized what they were witnessing. A member of a group protesting the imprisonment and imminent execution of Zulfikar Ali Bhutto had set himself on fire, giving the crowd an example of loyalty to his party's leader. Or had someone on the opposing side set him on fire? The smell of his skin and hair burning hung thick in the air.

The streets filled with shouts and screams, different groups hurled stones at one another, the tempest of protestors whipping into a frenzy. The bus rocked harder and harder. Stones, large and small, smacked the windows of the bus with loud cracks. A rock crunched against a window near where Victoria and her mother were seated, breaking the glass and hitting a man seated there. His eyes rolled back in his head, an open wound bled at his temple.

Victoria screamed and hid beneath her mother's seat. The gears of the bus groaned and little by little, it lurched forward, amid shouts from the fray that grew more panicked. Shrieks pierced through the mayhem as police in riot gear cut through the crowds like knives slicing through vegetables. They sprayed thick plumes of tear gas to push the crowd back, and in short order dispersed the unruly mobs.

As soon as the roadway cleared, the bus driver covered as much ground as possible, as quickly as possible. The roads out of Lahore were crowded, but their bus driver pushed the bus as hard as he could. After several hours, the bus arrived without further incident at the village where Victoria and her family lived.

At dinner that night, Victoria's mother told her husband about the events of the day. Her mother had grown frail these past two years, but today, her features seemed more gaunt than usual, and her voice trembled as she spoke.

Stunned, Ishaq sat quietly, rubbing his thick glasses on the hem of his shirt. "These are dangerous times."

"Why is this happening, father?" Victoria cried. "You said this would be a cultural shift, nothing more. Our lives are changing completely. Are culture and religion becoming the same law? It seems impossible!"

"You must change your attitude, my child."

"Why should I? They are the ones who are wrong. Executing the leader of Pakistan because they don't like his politics? What crime has he committed?"

"Victoria, if you don't change your attitude, it will turn into fear. That's what has happened to these people. They've grown overly fearful and have become afraid that their voice won't be heard. That leads people with similar voice to band together and become extreme in their cause. They've become so fearful, that they will no longer listen to reason or hear another side of the story. Their only option, in their minds, is violence."

"My voice has never been heard, father." Victoria's eyes narrowed in anger, her voice steeped in acrimony.

"I've been told to be quiet ever since I was a young child, not to ask questions about the Muslim religion, not to speak up when I've been insulted. Now, my father, do you think I am becoming an extremist? All because I love Jesus Christ?" Victoria slapped her palms on the table and stood in frustration.

"I am not your enemy, Victoria. Your mother and I understand the danger in this world far more than you do. Everything we've encouraged for you to do has been for your own good."

"That's gotten me nowhere, father."

"You haven't been killed or worse," her mother interjected, her tone dry. "I'd say that counts for something."

Victoria stomped away into the courtyard. The anger that had burned within her as a young child, rejected by her peers because of her religion, resurfaced. The devil that once sat on her shoulder encouraging her to be reckless and thoughtless with her speech and actions, now took residence once again.

She was struggling to find a way to forgive those who created the laws that now governed their country, laws that threatened to hurt or kill Christians because of their faith. As much as she tried, Victoria was unable to reach deep enough within herself to find the ability to forgive. The anger within her had taken on a palpable life of its own, and it would take more than young Victoria could offer at this moment to escape from it.

Prayer was all Victoria had to soothe the hatred that roiled within her. Today it felt impossible to hear anything Christ had to say. Victoria put her hands over her face and wept.

CHAPTER 17

"PURSUIT"

After the school break Victoria returned to Lucie Harrison High School. Lahore had been peaceful since the riots; she and her fellow students hoped there would be no more unrest. It was a false hope.

"Did you hear?" Nancy, a student in Victoria's class and one of her closest friends, burst into the main area of the boarding house where they lived. Victoria was sitting on her bed in her nightgown, brushing her hair. Her head snapped up when she heard the urgency in her classmate's voice.

"Jamat E Islami nearly killed Principal Anwar Barkat from Forman Christian College!"

Forman Christian College, a venerable liberal arts university, had been founded in 1864. It followed an American style curriculum, and had a reputation as one of the premiere learning institutions in Pakistan. Located on the banks of the Lahore Canal in Lahore, it was overseen and administered by the Presbyterian Church, until Prime Minister Bhutto was overthrown. When Zia came to power, the school was put under the administration of the government.

"What happened?" Victoria cried. Many of the girls swarmed around Nancy like buzzing bees hoping to hear more about her terrible news.

"I overheard the matrons talking," she continued. "They are afraid Jamat E Islami will come to assault other teachers here."

One of the new girls asked, "Who are they?"

"Where have you been? This is an angry movement. They want "complete Islam" in the way the Prophet Mohammed practiced Islam. The government wants to change any morality, politics, law or culture that is outside Islam, and convert those who follow any religion."

Victoria was alarmed at Nancy's news. She pushed her way through the small crowd of girls who'd gathered around to hear the rest of the story.

"Principal Barkat was a respected member of the community. Christians and Muslims alike listened to him and his teachings. What could have changed that?"

"Jamat E Islami," spat Nancy. "The matrons said they beat him so badly, they broke his nose and his back." Many girls gasped. Others clasped their hands in prayer.

Several of the youngest students burst into tears.

A somber mood pervaded the boarding house the next day as the girls prepared to leave the dormitory and attend classes. Several girls, including Victoria, gathered together to say a prayer for Barkat, who had been nearly killed for his Christian beliefs.

At school Victoria noticed several Muslim students who seemed to be smiling broadly, exuding a level of confidence she'd not noticed before. Was it because they saw the cultural shift, and believed the rapidly growing *Jamat E Islami* was succeeding? Didn't the Muslims hold enough control in Pakistan? Evil has a way of dividing even the closest of families, and schools.

Victoria worked as hard as she could to stifle her anger, to bury it deep. Today, she needed to send all the prayers she could to Christians who were being persecuted, rather than waste that energy on loathing some of her classmates. The hatred that rose within her against the Muslim students made her no better than they were.

The Christian girl had sought to educate herself about the beliefs and laws that governed Islam so that she could find understanding, instead of feeling loathing and anger.

In the afternoon, the matrons of the boarding house came back to Lucie Harrison High School to collect the students and bring them back to the dormitory. The students lined up, straight as an arrow, one behind the other. A matron in front led the way, and another followed behind, to ensure no one strayed. It was a time to be cautious. They took a footpath that spanned several blocks from the high school to their boarding house.

Victoria adjusted the sash she was now required to wear. All the girls wore white crisp ankle length *shalwar* pants, with knee length blue tunics. A smart white sash started at one shoulder and crossed the body and hung low. She'd been wearing this new outerwear since her return to school earlier in the year, but had not yet gotten used to it. Awkwardly, she always managed to trap a piece of the cloak under her shoes and trip.

As the girls began their walk back to the boarding house, a bus overflowing with men whipped around the corner. The bus windows were open and Victoria heard their raucous chants. She tried to ignore their insults, but as they chanted *"Jamat E Islami Zindabad",* "long live Jamaat e Isalmi". Her heart hammered in her chest and a cold trickle of sweat rolled down her back. She kept her head down, trying to become invisible, hoping the bus of aggressive fundamentalists would ignore the line of Christian girls walking down the street.

The brakes on the bus screeched as the bus skidded to an abrupt halt. Dust rose in great clouds and caught in Victoria's throat, making her cough.

"Run!" Matron Rose shouted from behind them. Born in Canada, the matron had worked for the police department in Toronto before becoming active in the Salvation Army. It seemed she had recognized the potential threat just as Victoria had, and was convinced that this busload of men would attack her charges.

The younger girls in the front began to scream. Each girl ran as fast as her legs could carry her. Matron Rose yelled at them to hurry. The men from *Jamat E Islami* jumped from their bus, shouting and laughing as they pursued everyone who was in the street.

Matron Rose reached the boarding house ahead of the students. She shouted for help to Mr. Moore, the boarding house keeper, and anyone else who could hear her.

The voice of the men grew louder as the mob bore down on the children. Matron Rose yanked open the heavy, eight-foot-wide, wrought iron gate and pushed each girl through as she arrived. Several men from the Salvation Army headquarters next door came out of their building and rushed to the aid of the girls. They wrapped their arms around them to shield them from the sticks, stones and garbage that were being hurled by the protestors. Some of the men from the boarding house carried the smaller girls in their arms, or on their backs, gripping the hands of others and leading them through the fray.

A stone narrowly missed Victoria as she tried to navigate the footpath in front of the boarding house. Her long cloak got twisted up beneath her, and she tripped. Her knee hit the edge of the footpath, and excruciating pain shot through her whole body. As she lay on the ground, other students rushed past her and something hit her on her back. The fundamentalists threw anything they could get their hands on at the frightened children. Laughing, howling, and hurling insults, the mob grew more unruly the closer they came to the boarding house.

"Can you walk?" Mr. Moore bent over and shielded Victoria with his body as stones and tree limbs bounced on the street around them.

"I don't know," she replied. Victoria removed her hand from the knee she was cradling; it was covered with blood. She continued to lie on the ground. Victoria knew she needed to be strong and resilient. She wouldn't get through this unless she forced herself to move, but the shouts around her froze her with fear. She couldn't move.

Then Mr. Moore picked Victoria up, cradled her in his arms and ran with her to the boarding house.

"Go directly to your dorm. Do not stay in the yard!" Matron Rose shouted above the din. The cries of the *Jamat E Islami* were rapidly escalating into a crescendo.

The girls filed into their sleeping quarters and huddled against the walls to protect themselves from shattered glass if a well aimed rock should break through a window.

"What do they want?" one of the younger students asked, as she clamped her hands over her ears, pressed her back against a wall, and rocked back and forth to comfort herself.

The matrons tried to calm the girls with their soft words, but the noise from outside grew louder still. Howling men climbed the boarding house gates, others banged on the wrought iron with sticks. Stones, large and small, pelted the sides of the boarding house and smacked against the windows while the girls huddled together in their dormitory, waiting out the aggressors, praying they wouldn't break down the gates.

After more than an hour, the members of *Jamat E Islami* moved on, taking their violence elsewhere. They left behind a dormitory full of frightened and confused Christian girls.

Slowly, the girls peeked out of the dorm room windows into their courtyard and watched as members of the Salvation Army assisted Mr. Moore and the gatekeeper in picking up the litter from the attack.

The school called Victoria's family, to explain what had happened and encourage her father to come to the school as quickly as he could. Ishaq left immediately.

One of the matrons had done her best to bandage Victoria's wound, and one of the men helped her to the dining area where she sat with her friends for their evening meal. Much of the meal was spent in silence with the girls still shaken and introspective about their afternoon. By the grace of God, they'd been spared unthinkable tragedy.

"How's your knee Victoria?" Matron Rose asked as Victoria was finishing up her food. Worry lines creased her face as she looked over Victoria carefully. On any normal day, Matron Rose's hair was twisted into a tight bun and her perfectly ironed clothing showed not a single wrinkle. Now, hair from her bun had escaped its pins and flowed down her back. Her clothing had trapped some of the dust from the streets. She had clearly been distressed by the threats her charges had faced at the hands of an opportunistic busload of fanatics.

"It's all right, I think." No longer burdened by the cumbersome cloaks she'd been forced to wear, Victoria showed Matron Rose her wound from beneath her uniform *shalwar* pants, still stained and torn from her fall. The gauze pad that had been applied less than an hour ago was already soaked with blood.

"You need to visit the nurse." Matron Rose said. She helped Victoria to stand and escorted her to the infirmary. The other girls gave sympathetic glances as she passed them on the way.

Victoria's leg had swollen to twice its normal size because of her injury. When the nurse pulled off the gauze pad, Victoria screamed in pain. The nurse furrowed her eyebrows in worry and pulled Matron Rose aside. They spoke for several moments in hushed tones. Matron Rose approached Victoria's bed.

Matron Rose held Victoria's hand as she explained. "It doesn't seem as if we can treat your injury properly here. We are going to need to send you to the hospital."

Victoria nodded her head. She bit her lip to keep it from quivering and hoped it would help keeping her tears from falling. She would try to be brave. She knew the injury was insignificant compared to what could have happened to her earlier.

Victoria's eyes felt heavy with sleep. She lay in the hospital bed after her treatment and the pain medication she'd been given had begun to take effect. She looked up as a shadowy figure entered her room and sat on the edge of her bed. A bit of remaining sunlight entered her room and glinted off a pair of thick glasses. Immediately, she recognized who it was.

"Father, it's you," Victoria whispered, her words slurring from the haze induced by her medication.

He took her hand in his, lifted it to his mouth and gently kissed it. "I am so grateful you are safe."

"My knee is fine, father."

"I am glad your knee is fine, but that wasn't all that I was referring to. You understand what could have happened to you today, don't you?"

Victoria nodded.

"That's why I am so grateful. The wound to your knee would heal, but other things could have happened to you today that would never heal. Our family might have been changed forever."

"I know father," Victoria said. She knew that the disgrace her father spoke of went well beyond the disgrace her family had already suffered. Ishaq squeezed her hand tightly.

Victoria understood the severity that the girls in her dormitory and the matrons narrowly avoided today. It was the one thing that would dishonor a Pakistani family more than any other; a girl or woman who had been defiled by rape. In Pakistan, rape is not so much a crime or an act of violence against women, as it is a tragedy that causes the woman and her family to suffer indignity and ostracism.

Victoria had heard of many instances of rape occurring during the unrest. Christian men protected their wives, daughters and mothers by sleeping in doorways to thwart any potential threat. Girls and women lived in daily fear and slept two to a bed to comfort one another. Horrible stories were told of mothers who killed their raped daughters to save their family the disgrace and indignity that would result if others discovered it.

Men sought to protect their women at all costs, even to the point of sacrificing their own lives to save the honor of the woman they were protecting. An unmarried woman or girl who was raped would never be married or accepted properly within the church because she was no longer a virgin. The victim would be relegated to a life of "sisterhood" or sent to do missionary work, because no one would marry her. A married woman who had been raped would be abandoned by her husband. If she were lucky enough to be married a second time, it would likely be to a widower or some-one who needed her to take care of him in his old age, or care for his children. It would be a marriage of convenience or pity, but never love.

In Pakistan, a woman who had been raped is valued as less than nothing. She must harbor her victimhood alone, suffer indignity and judgment in silence and pray for someone to be charitable toward her. Victoria said a prayer of thanksgiving to Jesus that she had not been violated, and neither had any of the women and girls she lived with.

Victoria didn't know when her father left. She dozed off to sleep thinking about how fortunate she had been, despite the great levels of fear she had suffered.

Matron Rose escorted Victoria back to the dormitory the following day. There, life had seemed to return to normal. Girls played soccer in the courtyard, shouting and laughing. Giggles emanated from the dorm rooms where they lived and slept. Soon, the sounds of trunks slamming, water running and the clang of lockers banging shut, permeated the dorm. Everyone gathered her belongings and packed for their summer break.

High school had ended for Victoria, and the next chapter of her life was waiting to begin.

CHAPTER 18
"WHOM CAN WE TRUST?"

Victoria and her family were thankful when she received word she had passed her exams, successfully completing high school. She knew what she had accomplished, but having it in writing made it more real. Unfortunately, her excitement was short lived.

Life in Pakistan remained volatile for Christians, and for Hindus as well; however, it seemed to Victoria that Christians were more targeted for attacks than Hindus. She often heard her parents talking in hushed tones while she pretended to sleep. Sometimes she overheard her father speaking to men he worked with in the *bethak* as she pretended to read a book:

> "These are dangerous times in our country... Where can we go when the violence starts...? Whom can we trust...?"

Across Pakistan, incidents like the angry attack at Victoria's boarding house became frequent occurrences, and many people weren't as lucky as she and her classmates. Students, administrators, other teachers and even strangers attacked Christian teachers in the newly nationalized schools. Schools with large populations of

Christian teachers were damaged; windows were broken, rocks thrown, and gates torn down.

Christian women, even those who attempted to follow the new cultural rules by wearing scarves, were accosted; insulting words were hurled at them. The biggest slight was for a man to forcibly remove a woman's scarf from her head, (Muslim or Christian), rendering her 'naked'. A man might kill another who insulted his wife, daughter or mother in such a manner. This sort of insult happened time and again, often resulting in violent and sometimes tragic altercations.

Fundamentalist Muslim groups whipped each other up into frenzies, instigating other fanatical groups by challenging them to see which group could achieve "complete Islam". Stalwart, peace loving Muslims protested these aberrations, but did not forcefully speak out against the persecution. They were in as much danger as the Christians.

Christians avoided calling undo attention to themselves, choosing to remain silent for fear of what might become of them and their families. Hindus, likewise, would not call attention to themselves by denouncing the fundamentalist groups. Living quietly in fear became a way of life for people in Pakistan.

The political turmoil of the Iran-Contra Affair between the Middle East and the United States further fueled the frenzied acts of the fundamentalist groups. It fed the Islamic distaste for the West and furthered the quest to eradicate the infidels.

In November and December 1979, Iranian Shiites seized the Grand Mosque in Mecca. Muslims in Pakistan were told on the radio that it was Americans and Europeans who had invaded the Muslim holy mosque. More protests erupted.

One of the most extreme fundamentalist groups besieged the consulate in Rawalpindi, then attacked churches in Lahore. Nuns and priests were beaten like animals in the streets. Mere months before those same nuns and priests had operated hospitals that cured even the extremists of their ills. The hospitals helped birth children of Pakistan, they taught and cared for the children, and had provided resources to impoverished families. The same people who had tirelessly served their community were now slaughtered because they were considered infidels.

Victoria considered these heinous acts abominable; intense anger festered within her. Despite her respect for the tenets of Islam, she could not fathom the way extremists interpreted the *Quran*, promoting violence as an acceptable way to encourage conversion.

One evening, Victoria, at home with her family, sat in the great room of their house. Her mother was resting while her sisters were sewing. With the radio turned on low, music provided a peaceful background as the family relaxed after supper. Victoria, however, was restless. The treatment of Christians in Pakistan had gotten to a point where she could no longer bear it. Her father made a 'humph' sound as he turned the page of the newspaper he was reading.

"More bad news at the hands of the Jamat E Islami?" Victoria asked, anger lacing her tone. "Or is it another extremist group that's taken to murdering innocent Christians?"

Ishaq folded the newspaper and placed it at his feet. He slid his thick glasses further up his nose and regarded his daughter carefully. "There is always bad news in the papers these days."

"What now?"

"My child, we live in controversial times. The best we can do is remain quiet, live our lives and remain faithful to Jesus."

"While the Muslims take control of everything? We should allow that to happen?"

"What choice do we have? We must remember the rules we live by. The Bible is our manual for how to live our lives. This is most important during these times."

"While they are free to use their *Quran* to justify these ghastly acts?"

"Yes. Just as we are free to interpret our Bible our way, they are free to interpret the Quran in their way. The *Quran* is as important to them as our Bible is to us."

"Even if they interpret the *Quran* wrong?"

"It's wrong to you."

"Then you are saying it's not wrong for them to behave this way in the name of Allah?"

Ishaq shrugged. "They don't believe so."

"Murder is wrong!" Victoria's face flushed in anger, her eyes wide open, her mouth taut.

Ishaq slowly took off his glasses and placed them on the small table close to him. "What does the *Quran* say about the treatment of infidels? You studied it at great lengths and even read it in Arabic."

Victoria sat back in her chair, eyes closed, remembering her classes in Muslim theology. "The *Quran* requires different punishments for Muslims and infidels. The punishment is more severe for infidels."

"Yes, but that's a small fragment of it, isn't it?"

"Young boys are told that above all else, they are soldiers of Allah and can use their swords to kill. Many are taking this literally. They are told that killing a Christian is rewarded with a direct visa to Paradise where they will be showered with 72 virgins."

"So, the desire for women becomes a tool for obedience?"

"That is what some false teachers tell them. The *Quran* does not agree with their interpretation," Victoria said.

"Are you saying the *Quran* is not wrong, but the interpretation is?"

"Yes, that is what I mean."

From her studies, she had learned that women are powerless in Muslim Pakistan. They are told to shield their faces and their bodies to avoid being considered desirable. Education is discouraged. Women are to serve their family as matriarchs by raising children, cooking, cleaning and serving the needs of the family patriarch and breadwinner. Sexual deviance of any sort is exposed and punishable by death.

"Some scholars of Islam strive to bring hateful interpretations of Islam into the community and force them into law. This can be dangerous," Victoria's father said. "My father, when he was living, warned us of this possibility."

Although Victoria's revered grandfather had passed away many years before, Victoria still remembered his teachings. She missed him dearly, and would have loved to hear his commentary on the current state of affairs in Pakistan.

"Muslim women are not even allowed to serve as nurses in the hospitals," Victoria continued.

"Exactly," her father replied. "A Muslim woman would not be allowed to see a man in a state of undress. That would not be considered respectable."

"It is respectable for a Christian woman to be a nurse."

"It is. A Christian woman does not have the same religious rules governing her as a Muslim woman does. A Christian woman is encouraged to serve others by whatever means she can. When a Christian woman becomes a nurse, and helps heal others, she is acting Christ-like. For a Muslim woman, covering herself and serving her family members is acting as the Prophet Mohammed would expect. Both women are trying to be faithful to God."

"I suppose they are. But the extremists..." Victoria paused and sighed. "They are taking the beautiful tenets of the *Quran* and creating such ugliness from them."

"There is always pain and great suffering before a period of reformation. It is a well-documented part of history and it will continue until the end of time."

Ishaq picked up his glasses and pushed them back up the bridge of his nose and looked at Victoria squarely. "There will be a reformation in Islam. There was in Christianity. Before this, the Crusades created many years of bloodshed. A teacher of mine once said that more people have died for the love of their God than for anything else. While many have, in the twentieth century, this turned out not to be true. Godless human beings are infected with the stain of sin; this will always be the case. Both good and evil reside within the human heart."

"I know most Muslims are good people. I don't understand why they support this fanaticism."

Ishaq was silent for a while as he stared into space. Then he said, "I think some Muslims in Pakistan believe that this level of radicalization shows power and control over "outsiders," and is a positive thing for the Muslim community. They genuinely feel these acts will ultimately lead to the betterment of the new nation we are building."

"Really father? Eradicating the Christian schools with such good reputations that even Muslims wanted to send their children there to be educated? Eliminating Christian run hospitals with such excellent care and treatment facilities that Muslims chose them over state run hospitals because of their reputation?" Victoria set her jaw.

"They deprive their communities of excellent education and health care. How does that serve for the betterment of their community?"

"You have to look at it through their eyes. Muslim teachers say Christians are infidels, even if they do bring wonderful things to the Muslim communities in Pakistan."

"Even the liberal Muslims think this way?" Victoria asked.

"Well, some of them may feel differently." Her father chuckled. "I read of a Pakistani Cabaret club where liberal Muslims, Christians, doctors, lawyers and even Colonels in the army would convene."

"At the same time?" Victoria asked, a blush creeping up on her cheeks. She was embarrassed to speak of something like a cabaret club with her father.

"Oh yes," he grinned. "All together at once."

Feeling bold, Victoria said, "Well, it's good to know that wine, women and cigars can bridge the differences between politics and religions. If all else fails, at least we have that."

Ishaq's eyes widened and Victoria feared he might strike her for crossing a line. Instead, her father surprised her and burst into laughter. "There is that. Yes, there is."

CHAPTER 19
"AN ATTEMPT AT CONVERSION"

"*Zeenat!*" Victoria's mother called.

Zeenat was the house cleaner or 'sweeper' who had worked for Victoria and her family for several years. In Pakistani culture, sweeper work was considered a menial job, work that only those with a low zat would fill. Many of these jobs were taken by low-caste Christians because of the strictly limited employment in more preferred occupations.

Zeenat was on her hands and knees scrubbing the tiled kitchen floor, using a wooden brush with stiff bristles. She dropped the brush into the bucket of water that sat beside her, pressed a hand to the small of her back and stood slowly. Beads of sweat had collected along her graying hairline; Zeenat wiped her wet hands onto her apron and approached Victoria's mother with a weary smile. "Yes, Madam?"

Her mother placed a slim, undernourished arm around Victoria's shoulders and gave her as great a smile as she could these days. There were many days as of late where her mother couldn't even get out of bed.

"My daughter has graduated from high school! She has honorably passed her exams and plans to attend college in the fall." Her mother did not often boast of Victoria's accomplishments. Zeenat blushed at the compliment.

"Praise Jesus!" Zeenat exclaimed and raised her hands above her head in exultation. She enveloped Victoria in a great hug. Zeenat's frame was thin but she was far from frail. Her clothing, damp from sweat and exertion, clung to her body. Victoria quickly pulled back from Zeenat's strong embrace, taken aback by the hard-working woman's odor. In fear of offending her, Victoria instead took Zeenat's coarse hands and held them tightly.

Zeenat's strong, dark hands were rough and weathered from her frequent scrubbing, brushing and sweeping. They contrasted sharply with Victoria's light, soft skin and she realized that Victoria hardly knew the Christian woman who had cleaned their home for so many years.

After their embrace, the story of Jesus healing a man with leprosy came to Victoria's mind. A man, shunned for being unclean and disease ridden, approached Jesus, asking to be healed. Jesus did not just stand apart from the leper, He touched the unclean man and cured him of his ailment.

Just then, Victoria's maternal grandmother entered the great room from the courtyard and cast a stern look at Zeenat. Zeenat quickly lowered her eyes and dropped Victoria's hands. She backed up a couple of steps into the kitchen, dropped to her knees, and dipped her hand back into the bucket to retrieve the brush she'd been using.

"Grandmother!" Victoria admonished.

"I'll have none of that young lady." She shook her head and gave Victoria the same stern stare she had given their sweeper. "People need to learn their place."

"Mother," Victoria's mother interjected. She took her mother's arm and pulled her into the great room out of earshot of their sweeper. "This is my home. Zeenat is a Christian woman who deserves respect."

"Anyone who cleans a toilet is unclean. I don't want her dirty hands upon my granddaughter."

Victoria's mother sighed. "Mother, I understand why you feel that way, but I don't. I don't think a person's job has anything to do with their character. I judge people based on their character."

"That is your opinion. I, however, will remain out of your sweeper's presence until she has completed her filthy tasks." Her grandmother sat in a wooden chair, arms crossed. In her mind, the discussion was over.

Victoria had been aware of her grandmother's opinions over the years, but having lived away at boarding school, she'd rarely witnessed them in action. Now that she had, Victoria felt a greater respect for Zeenat's continued kindness and the work she did for her family. She guessed no employer treated Zeenat as kindly as her mother.

Victoria's grandmother was a convert to Christianity, just as her paternal grandfather had been. Converting to Christianity from Hinduism was less of an insult than converting from Islam, in terms of the overall caste system of the country. There remained some stigmas that resulted from the caste system that Hindus did support. Sweepers belong to a very low caste, and as a result are regarded as unclean. Victoria's grandmother would not go anywhere near a sweeper because of that.

Victoria's mother, however, saw things differently. Whenever Zeenat was cleaning, her mother would often sit and talk with her, engaging in conversation that often resulted in boisterous laughter. Her mother always gave Zeenat a Christmas gift during the holidays, or slipped her an extra treat like a fresh mango as she was leaving for the day.

Victoria's mother treated everyone she met respectfully, Christians, Hindus and Muslims alike. Victoria, through her mother, came to understand how important that was, and she made it a point to mimic that in her own life. From the way she had been treated as a child, Victoria understood that even the smallest token of kindness went a long way to healing even the deepest of wounds. Through her mother's example she began to recognize the closeness she was feeling to her own faith. When she saw the kindness shown to their sweeper, she'd felt the presence of the Holy Spirit.

Victoria's summer passed quickly. She had been accepted to the local government college near Sahniwal, a smaller city, not far from the city of Lahore, where Victoria and her family continued to live. Her father had arranged with a co-worker to share the task of driving their daughters to and from the college in Sahniwal.

The first day of college, Victoria emerged from her home and walked toward the pickup truck parked at the curb in front of her home. A girl a little older than she sat in the passenger seat. Victoria could see only her eyes since she wore a *burka*, but those eyes seemed kind and gentle. Victoria breathed a sigh of relief hoping she would be free of any harsh judgment passed on her first day of school.

She smoothed down the crisp white *kameez* of her uniform, the one she'd been accustomed to wearing in high school, and walked toward the curb, a smile on her face. She had decided she would do all she could to befriend the girl with whom she was driving to school, and try to look at everything with less passion.

The driver, a Pakistani man with a thick mustache, glared at Victoria. One look at her and the man driving the car had made a scathing judgment of her. An angry flush began to creep up her neck. Unconsciously, Victoria's fists clenched at her side.

The man emerged from his vehicle, his hands raised in the air. "Where is your father?" he demanded. *"I must speak with him at once."* Victoria knew this man held a higher government position than her father and reminded herself that she must not lash out.

"I will get him," Victoria kept her eyes downcast so he wouldn't see the flush in her cheeks. The anger in this gentleman's eyes frightened Victoria.

Hearing the man's shouts, Ishaq emerged from the house. "Naeem," her father called to his co-worker, a smile on his face. "Good morning my friend." Ishaq brushed past his daughter on his way to greet his co-worker and under his breath he whispered, *"Go inside. Now."* Victoria quickly obeyed. Her nervousness gave way to fear, and she felt herself shaking. She ran into the kitchen to find her mother while her father spoke outside with his co-worker.

"Victoria!" her mother exclaimed scanning her from her head to her feet. "You aren't dressed properly. Where is your *chaddar?"* Dark circles ringed her mother's eyes, the hollows of her cheeks more pronounced than ever.

"This is what I wore to high school. It is my uniform. I haven't changed it in any way. How is this no longer acceptable?" Victoria protested.

Her mother sighed and a weary look settled in her eyes. She yanked a *chaddar* from a hook near the entry way door. Victoria had often seen her mother wear the long shawl made of a soft, thin cotton in a vibrant pink with beautiful gold and white flowers handstitched into the fabric. The piece was beautiful, but she did not like the reason her mother was handing it to her.

"Put this on." Her mother thrust the *chaddar* at her. Victoria heard the front door open and knew her father had come back into the house. She heard his shoes on the tile floor.

"I'm not Muslim," Victoria protested and crossed her arms across her chest.

"This defiance will get you nowhere," her father bellowed from behind her. "Wear the *chaddar* or do not go to college. Your choice."

Victoria cringed inside, but she snatched the *chaddar* from her mother and draped it over her head. She wrapped it careful-ly around her shoulders so that it wouldn't extend too far to the ground where she might trip over it. Ever since her accident when she ran from the *Jamat E Islami* procession, Victoria had taken great care with the length of her clothing. The unsightly scar that still crossed her knee reminded her of it each day.

"You may remove it when you get to school but while you are in the presence of men besides your father and brothers, you must keep it on." Her mother pressed a hand to Victoria's back, prodding her out the door.

Her eagerness to further her education outweighed the insult she felt at having to wear this heavy and cumbersome clothing, so she shuffled awkwardly back to the pick-up truck. Naeem stood with his arms crossed in front of him, tapping his foot. When he saw Victoria emerge from her home in the "proper" attire, he nodded his head abruptly and sat back inside the vehicle.

Victoria shut the door after sliding onto the seat.

"I'm Anam," the girl in the front passenger seat said with a bright smile as she turned to face Victoria.

Victoria returned her smile grateful for the kindness she had shown her.

Anam's brows furrowed. "What is your zat?"

"I am Christian."

Anam nodded. "That explains your Christian name, then." Anam turned forward in her seat. After a few moments, she turned back to look at Victoria. "You don't look Christian."

"What are Christians supposed to look like?" Victoria asked.

"All Christians I know have dark skin. Yours is light, like mine and other Muslims." Anam gave Victoria a quick smile and turned back in her seat again.

Anger roiled within her. She clenched her teeth so she wouldn't say something rude and argumentative. Just like that, Victoria had been transported back in time to her first school experience. She half thought Anam would turn back around, point a finger at her and yell, "*Paleed*". Instead, it was worse.

With great pride Anam declared, "I wish you would accept Islam, and you will have the best of both worlds, here and in eternity. If you accept Islam, a whole new world will be available to you."

As she spoke Anam casually glanced at Victoria over her shoulder, as if she were rattling off a list of things that were needed from the market for dinner that evening.

Victoria clenched her jaw even tighter, forcing back the insults she was tempted to spew, criticizing Islam. Somehow, she resisted, and stifled her voice. Again.

Her father would be proud that she had not caused a scene, but inside, she felt disgusted with herself for not arguing for her beliefs."

Sheepishly she said, "Right now, Anam, I am worried about the 'worlds' of college."

⇒+ +⇐

That evening at dinner, Victoria expressed her concerns.

"I don't want to go back."

"Why the change of heart?" Ishaq asked.

"I don't like wearing the *chaddar,* and that girl, Anam, insulted me. She told me that I look Muslim and then tried to convert me to Islam. Am I going to have to endure this every day?"

"Be sensible, Victoria. Religion doesn't have to be the topic of conversation."

"Anam made it the topic of conversation and I fear she will continue to do so until she converts me."

"Then ask her politely not to discuss religion. It's not wrong to do that."

"I don't like her father either. I have to ride in his car every day, and he scares me."

Victoria pushed some rice about on her plate with her *naan,* her bottom lip sticking out in a childish pout. She had grown into a young woman, a capable adult, yet those old childhood feelings of rejection would not let go of her.

Ishaq sighed. "Victoria, please push your feelings aside and focus instead on your studies. At this point, you don't have much of a choice."

Victoria thought she might as well wear the *chaddar* across her lips, and stuff the end of it in her mouth. Everyone around her tried to dismiss her, and silence her voice. It irritated her that it might be best not to have any opinions. She was an educated, devout woman, cautioned to say nothing at all, not to her peers, her parents or those who rejected her.

Victoria knew that if she was asked to leave the college, she would have to submit to marriage with someone of her parents choosing. This she was not ready to do.

Only one day in school and a wave of anxiety ran through the young woman. She began thinking about her failed engagement to William. Not a day passed that Victoria didn't feel inferior because of the dishonor her family had faced. Then, a further insult from the young man: Victoria's parents had learned that William had moved to Saudi Arabia. Any hope that Victoria had of reconciling with William was crushed. That news had left her mother confined to her bed, consumed with worry for the future of her daughters.

She couldn't imagine marrying any of the men in her village, not that there had been offers. Most of the men were considerably older than her, men with whom she held nothing in common. Some were stand-offish and serious and would prove to be a disastrous match for the outgoing, opinionated Victoria. William had been different. He greeted everyone with a smile, had a hearty laugh and was a friend to everyone. He had been a good match. Victoria still couldn't understand what she had done to drive him away.

The tears of sadness that welled in her eyes competed with the anger that ran through her heart. Victoria became anxious, at times inconsolable. So many competing emotions fought for room inside, that she didn't know what to do. Now, she pushed her plate aside and stepped into the courtyard for an evening stroll, hoping to walk off some of those painful feelings.

CHAPTER 20

"AN OFFENSE"

"Did you think about what we discussed? Islam and eternal life?"

It was the second day of college and they had hardly been in the car for ten minutes when Anam spun about in her seat and began hammering Victoria with questions. Would this girl's attempts at converting her never cease?

"Please, Anam, let's not discuss religion anymore."

"Or what? Are you threatening me?" Anam tossed her head and glared at Victoria.

"Of course not," Victoria raised a hand to her chest offended at the implication. "I am happy to be a Christian and I wish to remain Christian."

"Clearly you don't know enough about Islam, then. Otherwise, you wouldn't feel that way." Anam's glare disappeared and she employed the benign smile she used while attempting to evangelize her passenger. She felt as if Anam literally had two faces.

"I know plenty about Islam," Victoria returned. She wanted to tell Anam how, in high school, she had achieved the best marks in her Islamic studies classes, grades higher than her Muslim classmates.

"I'll bring you some books to study." Anam turned and faced forward again in her seat, an indication that she had finished trying to influence Victoria for the day. For the second day in a row, Victoria seethed during her morning commute.

That day Victoria had decided to wear a rosary around her neck. Although she and her family weren't Catholic, the rosary was a gift that had been passed down and had found its way to Victoria. It was beautifully crafted, made of soft rosewood beads, with a silver crucifix hung from a medallion of the Virgin Mary. She hoped that keeping a symbol of her faith close to her heart would help her deflect any unkindness, and allow her to focus on her studies.

"You can't wear that," a girl in Victoria's class sneered at her and cast an ugly look at the rosary as Victoria sat down beside her.

Victoria fingered the crucifix. "Why not? You have a separate room where you can pray. It seems only fair that I be allowed to wear a symbol of my religion."

The government administered the college Victoria attended, and Christian teachers were not permitted. All instructors were Muslim, and the cultural shift that had occurred in Pakistan required appropriate dress and prayer time.

"Take it off, it's offensive."

Victoria's mouth gaped open, angered that this girl dare call the crucifix offensive. It was her intolerant attitude that was truly offensive. Victoria opted to visit the principal's office to plead her case.

"It's a beautiful rosary, but it's best if you wear it inside your shirt."

"Why? I don't understand what the problem is!" Victoria protested. She was unwilling to admit that inside, she knew exactly what the problem was.

The principal lowered her head and beckoned Victoria closer. She was kind and wise. Quietly she said, "You're not in Lahore anymore. It's not nearly as liberal here as it was there."

Victoria begrudgingly relented, realizing that she could be beaten or worse because of her religion; that would have been true even in a liberal city like Lahore. Here, in this small city, people were far less tolerant, making the risks even greater. Was this the world she would forever be forced to endure? One where she would never be able to display her faith freely?

She wondered if she would always have to hide her feelings and her faith, whether under her shirt or in her heart.

Because of Victoria's insistent pleading, her father finally gave her permission to live at a boarding house with several other Christian women. She rather expected she would be insulted at school, but at least she wouldn't have to endure the intolerant Anam's futile efforts to convert her. With her Christian friends at the boarding house, Victoria found the strength to complete her first year of college.

She returned home for the summer and almost immediately began to study the Bible. She also continued her study of Islam, still struggling to understand why Muslims were so intolerant of Christians.

"It is not easy dealing with an intelligent child," Victoria's mother said to her father late one evening when she thought her daughter was asleep.

"I pray she will become a teacher. That way she will be able to express herself and allow her students to form their own opinions. Preferably she will be a math teacher."

Ishaq chuckled. "Yes, there is little room for philosophical discussion if she teaches math!" Then he had a thought. "Maybe we can enroll her in the United Bible Theological College for the summer."

"And fill her head with more religious fervor?"

"I know you are frustrated, but our daughter has an inquisitive mind. Perhaps if she goes to the Bible college she will find answers to some of her questions. Neither you nor I can give her adequate answers any longer."

Victoria's mother agreed. "Her Christian teachers have always held great influence over her. Perhaps they can help her manage her anger."

CHAPTER 21
"A FAITH MISSION REVEALED"

Victoria could barely contain her excitement as she traveled by bus to the United Bible Theological College (UBTC) in Gujranwala – a good sized city in Punjab. She eagerly anticipated the opportunity to strengthen her faith and heal her mind. She was grateful to her parents for their thoughtfulness.

United Presbyterian missionaries from North America funded the Seminary, and the UBTC. They did so out of compassion for their fellow Pakistani Christians. Victoria had heard of the school's reputation as an outstanding theological institute; she was most impressed by the school's grand library. Thousands of books lined the great gilded library as far as the eye could see. Men of faith taught the origins of Christianity in English and Urdu, something that impressed Victoria. Immediately, she knew she would fit in.

She also felt that having this opportunity for the summer would give her the strength she needed to continue her studies and graduate from the college.

One of Victoria's first classes at UBTC was about training girls to become Bible Teachers, an effort to make Christian women equally involved in evangelism and in teaching young children.

She learned more about Muslim young people, and about herself. It was through her participation in this course that Victoria began to understand why Muslim youth were willing to martyr themselves.

She was taught that younger Muslims of Pakistan often came from situations where they were scarred by conflict at an early age. Threats of war with India, violent religious conflicts, influence children. Their anger was transformed when they discovered a new feeling of love and acceptance in Islam. That complex emotional attachment to their religion makes it easier for them to martyr themselves in the name of Allah. This was a revelation to Victoria.

But she also learned about herself. Pakistan of the 1970s was a difficult place to grow up. She understood better the challenge she was having, converting from an angry human being to a loving Christian. At UBTC she was learning new lessons for life that would help her, but she knew that taming her rebellious nature would continue to be a challenge. As a young Christian woman, she chastised herself and remained penitent for the mean streak she harbored.

Victoria often felt uneasy about her inability to be continually loving and considerate; she wondered if she would ever be free to love everyone. Even now, as a student at the Bible College, she found it difficult to accept her own faults and flaws, and to stay willing to change.

Her comparative religions class helped her explore new depths in her Christian faith; she felt comfortable asking her questions without feeling foolish.

"Let's talk about King David," Professor Nasir began. "What humble beginnings did the great King David came from?"

"He was a shepherd," Victoria called out.

Professor Nasir smiled. "He was. A lowly shepherd boy. His caste so low, he didn't seem to have one." Many students nodded. "He was underestimated. Why?"

"He was a boy," someone from the back of the room called.

"Yes, youth. And?"

"He was poor," called out another student.

"Yes, because he was poor he was cast off and considered irrelevant."

"Then he became strong," Victoria said. "He wasn't weak and insignificant. He grew mighty and strong because of his trust in God."

"Very good point, Victoria." Professor Nasir smiled at her then said, "We all are like the great King David." Murmurs sputtered through the room.

"I know, I know," Professor Nasir held up his hands. "It seems improbable but let's look at our faith for just a moment. As Pakistani Christians, you are taught by society that you are irrelevant. You are forced to be poor by the jobs that are available to you as Christians. Because you choose to turn the other cheek when your religion is insulted, you are considered weak. Have any of you ever felt any or all of those things as a Christian here in Pakistan?"

Many students nodded their heads or raised their hands. Victoria looked about the room and saw at least twenty other people who felt the same way she did. She felt conflicted; she didn't know whether to rejoice or to be angry that the society in which they lived had forced others to endure what she had.

Professor Nasir continued, "You will not always feel this way. You are followers of the faith, you believe in Jesus Christ, and you have endured suffering because of your love for Him. Your faith will keep you strong in life and in death, you will become glorified and live in the Kingdom of Heaven."

Tears welled up in Victoria's eyes. She had suffered all her life for her love of Christ. Perhaps one whose faith wasn't so strong might be swayed because it was easier than enduring the persecution that formed such a large part of a Christian's life in Pakistan. Victoria was thankful that her own faith had not waivered. The potential was there for the pain to impact her relationship with the Lord.

"What about the Apostle Peter?" Victoria called out.

"What about him?"

"His faith was weak even as an apostle of Jesus. He denied Christ three times, just as Jesus said he would."

"His faith grew even stronger as a result. Peter denied his faith out of fear for his own life. How many of you would do the same?"

"Never!" Victoria insisted, but the murmurs that swelled around her indicated that some might have acted as Peter had. Victoria herself, with her light skin tone and her keen knowledge of Islam, could have easily blended in with the Muslim population. Her life could have been so much simpler had she not declared her Christianity so boldly to everyone around her. Her parents had repeatedly warned her of exactly that, and now she finally understood.

"We all have our challenges in our lives and in our faith," Professor Nasir said. He walked up and down the rows of desks as he spoke, looking at each student as he spoke. "Peter had his challenges and Jesus forgave his faults. He will forgive any of you for the same. Christ has given us each special gifts, and expects different things of each of us; he challenges us in unique ways. Once you mature in your faith, you will know what you must do for Him."

"I know what I must do for Him," Victoria confessed. She told the class that her grandfather had converted to Christianity from Islam. "My grandfather would hand me his Bible and I would read it to my brothers, sisters and cousins. He would say to me, 'You are to give your life for Him who gave His life for you.' He explained that no matter what suffering I had to endure, I was to dedicate my life to Christ and His teachings."

Those moments when her grandfather Talib had held her on his lap and taught her Bible verses, would remain with Victoria throughout her entire life. Her grandfather had helped shape her unwavering faith in Christ.

"Wonderful!" Professor Nasir clasped his hands together prayerfully and nodded at Victoria. "But, do you sometimes find yourself falling short of that?"

"Only when I become so angry at the Muslims. I do not want to love Muslims, even if the Bible tells me I should. I find it difficult to love those who persecute me."

"You love your grandfather."

"Of course! He was everything to me."

"He was Muslim."

"He was Christian," Victoria corrected.

"Not always." Professor Nasir put a pointer finger to his lips and regarded Victoria thoughtfully. "He was once a Muslim but you were still able to love him. Did you love him because he was Christian?"

"No, it was because he was my grandfather and a wonderful man."

"What lived inside him is what made the difference. His kindness, his love for others, that was what mattered.""

"Of course!"

"That is how it should be for everyone we meet. We must not judge people based on what we see on the outside. Instead, we must look past things such as religious labels, skin tones, gender, age, economic status to see what lives within. That is how we fulfill Christ's teachings."

Professor Nasir stood in front of Victoria, kindness in his eyes. "Perhaps one of those Muslims you find so difficult to love may be someone God wants to bring to Jesus. Maybe God is using you to share with that person the love that will transform him."

Victoria nodded. Professor Nasir had revealed one thing she had fought to reconcile in herself. How could she be the best

Christian she could be when her heart was filled with hatred toward Muslims?

It was then that she recognized she needed to create a mission statement for herself, a faith mission. As a Christian, it was her obligation to love and serve others as she would love herself, including Muslims. It would be her purpose, her mission in life, to learn to love and serve Muslims.

She did not realize how well that would turn out.

CHAPTER 22
"IN MOURNING"

Victoria studied at United Bible Theological College each of the summers throughout her time in college. In doing so, she found the faith to persevere through the taunts and angry stares of many of the students at her college, and graduated with degrees and high marks in math, computer sciences and economics. She became a well-educated woman during a time when Pakistani culture put up barriers to women.

Shortly after Victoria finished her courses at the Bible College, her mother passed away. She lost the woman she loved, confided in, and consulted for everything a young girl needed to know. It was a hard time for the whole family; the sorrow created a deep scar in Victoria's heart.

Zeenat, the family's' sweeper, brought them figs carefully wrapped in cheesecloth, with a handwritten note expressing her sympathies. Victoria accepted the simple gift, knowing it was something the sweeper could ill afford. Defying the norms of her community, Victoria embraced Zeenat. In tears, she held onto the scrubwoman as if her mother might return to her if she clung to the old woman long enough. As Victoria mourned her mother,

Zeenat's kindness found a special place in the sorrowing girl's heart, and provided her with much needed spiritual support.

Victoria recalled how her mother had treated everyone with respect. Her example helped her daughter to more fully understand the importance of love. It reinforced to Victoria what her faith mission was about, as she strove to mimic her mother's selfless giving in her life. Even the smallest token of kindness could heal the deepest of wounds.

After the loss of her mother, Victoria spent more time at home with her father, often cooking the family meal. One evening when they were home alone, she served her father a steaming bowlful of *daal (lentils)*. Her father scooped up a great mound of the lentils with a chunk of *naan* bread and closed his eyes as he savored the stew. Victoria had tried her best to make it the same way her mother had, but feared she fell short of her mother's abilities in the kitchen.

"Just like your mother's," Ishaq whispered. Victoria blushed at the compliment. She looked back at her father and opened her mouth to say something. Then, she noticed his eyes grow distant, and a soft moan passed his lips. Victoria thought she saw the haunted look of loneliness and grief overcome him, so she chose to remain silent and leave him alone with a memory of his wife.

As much as her father tried to hide his grief, Victoria could see that her mother's passing had left him lost and alone. He had loved her deeply; Victoria noticed that he would sit in his chair in the *bethak*, and stare into space, a look of longing on his face. Her father's face showed how much he missed his wife, but it also affected his gait. He had once walked confidently and upright, but there was now a hesitation to his step, and a slight bow to his back. It was as if the rod that had kept him upright had been snatched from him. He was forced to learn how to go through life on his own.

Uncharacteristically, anger radiated from him. That night a stern look occupied his countenance, his lips curled in a scowl. The anger that raged through him had taken residence in his daughter as well. In their own ways, they blamed William for Susan's passing. He was the first to bring it up.

"If only he hadn't made up some poor excuse for not marrying you," Ishaq mumbled, a fist pounding the table.

Victoria's heart hammered in her chest. As it had many nights since her mother's death, William would be the topic of dinner conversation. "Father..."

"Your mother was consumed with worry because of his feckless decision. He is the reason she lost herself with a grief so profound that it stole her soul."

Victoria felt the anger growing within her. "I understand, father. I feel that he is nothing more than a criminal and I pray I never set my eyes on him again."

Her father nodded. "We agree then, my daughter." Her father dropped his piece of *naan* to the table and clasped his daughter's hand in his. "I have some news for you, my daughter."

Victoria's head snapped up. The lines and creases in her father's face had deepened considerably these past several months, ever since Susan had left his side. Beyond the anger, she now saw a glimmer of hopefulness glinting in his eyes.

"I have been approached by your Uncle. He's arranged a marriage for you with a Christian man. He's an older man, he's never been married but he is willing to overlook your current situation. I've accepted the proposal."

Victoria sucked in a breath. She had given up all thoughts of marriage. This proposal came as a shock.

Victoria and her father ate the rest of the meal in silence, each lost in their own pain. While Victoria knew her father remained hopeful regarding this new husband, the man proved to be an unacceptable match.

CHAPTER 23

"A MISSIONARY"

A t dinner that evening, Victoria was no longer able to keep her good news to herself. She had been searching for a job. It hadn't been long before she'd received an offer that she wanted to take.

"Father, I've taken a job in Rawalpindi at a mainstream school. I will be teaching computer science."

"Praise Jesus!" Ishaq exclaimed. "I am so proud!" She couldn't ignore the slight tremor that shook his hands as he held them out for her to clasp.

"Thank you, father. As a Christian woman teaching in a high school where most of the students and teachers are Muslim, I feel this is a great opportunity for me."

"You are beginning a teaching career at an optimum time," Ishaq agreed, chewing on some *dhal*. "Each day more Afghani refugees from Kabul come into Pakistan and they are a very educated group. Did you know their schooling requires they learn several languages? French and English?"

"Farsi, too," added Victoria.

"They will create an interesting blend with Pakistani culture."

"I think so too." Victoria passed her father a plate of watermelon, lightly salted, but her father held up a hand in refusal.

"I feel as if I am a missionary of sorts," Victoria said pushing her empty bowl of stew away. Her father looked at her, eyes raised curiously.

"I am one of the few women who know computer sciences, so they had little choice but to hire me when I applied for the job."

Ishaq nodded and the traces of a smile crossed his face. "I am not surprised, Victoria. I am sure you had quite a way with them, convincing them of your abilities."

"I am qualified. More than that, I would like to honor the missionaries that came here and taught me."

"Your Christian teachers had always influenced you in a positive manner."

"I would like to do the same for these children coming from Afghanistan, and for the Pakistani children who wish to learn. So many of our wonderful missionaries had to leave us after the hostage crisis in Iran. I see this as my turn to take what has been taught me, and to share it with the students I have the privilege to teach."

"May God bless you, Victoria and lead you on the righteous path." Ishaq planted a kiss on his daughter's forehead and took his half-eaten plate to the kitchen.

Even through the continued sorrow that consumed her father at the death of his beloved wife, Victoria could sense that her father approved of her new path. He'd always been her champion as he encouraged her education and supported her on her life's journey. She did not know how quickly her first missionary opportunity would occur, but she had prepared herself for a servant future, believing strongly that the love of the Holy Spirit would empower her efforts.

Victoria started her teaching career in the early 1990s in Rawalpindi/Islamabad. Rawalpindi, together with its twin city,

Islamabad, comprises the fourth largest city in Pakistan. Situated almost 100 miles northwest of Lahore, the two cities are well known for their technical and vocational education. Engineers, welders, metallurgists and workers in the telecommunications industry get their education there.

Rawalpindi is also considered a hub for Pakistan's tourism industry, so there are opulent hotels, famous restaurants, museums and art galleries, as well. Ayub National Park and the Purana Qilla Market, famous for their breathtaking, beautifully crafted bridal gowns, are in Rawalpindi. It was a wonderful city in which to work.

After partition in 1947, Rawalpindi-Islamabad became the headquarters for the Pakistan Army; and the British influence, particularly in education, remained. In her new position, Victoria taught in a private English high school. The school was affiliated with the Cambridge School system, the system the British had introduced during the time of occupation. Rawalpindi-Islamabad was considered a wealthy city and the students who attended the school came from wealthier families who could afford private school instruction.

Familiar with the workings of private schools through her own educational experience, Victoria fit in well. She taught computer science, which allowed her to temper her philosophical questions, and religious differences she might have had with the families of her students.

Almost immediately, Victoria noticed a boy named Saqib, who, with his younger brother Abid, were new to the school and seemed to have a difficult time adjusting. Their grades in math and computer sciences were poor, but even as a first-year teacher, Victoria could tell their troubles in school went well beyond not understanding the subject matter.

"Saqib, are you all right?" Victoria asked, stopping the young man one day on his way to lunch.

Saqib kept his head down, his eyes to the ground and mumbled, "Yes, madam."

"If there's something you need help with, I am available. Please, ask."

"I will, madam." The boy responded and still would not look up.

Victoria went into the staff room where the teachers gathered to eat their lunch while students took their break. As she ate, Victoria worried about young Saqib and his brother. She didn't understand what it was about these boys that had made them stand out to her. She did know she needed to step in and help these young Muslim boys.

"Are you familiar with the new students, Abid and Saqib?" Victoria asked one of her fellow teachers.

"Yes, I know of them." Teacher Anum said.

"Their grades in math and computer science are poor. I was wondering if their grades were poor in other subjects as well."

"It's sad, but yes."

"It is something beyond school, then."

"They're refugees from Afghanistan." Anum said, and seemed surprised that Victoria was unaware of that.

"Thank you for telling me." Victoria said, registering further concern. This new information made sense to her. Displacement, and fear would create problems for a young child; Victoria was a product of that herself.

In the courtyard that afternoon, Victoria watched as the children were dismissed. She noticed an exceptionally beautiful, tall woman approach the boys. She looked as if she could grace the covers of Paris' high fashion magazines. The haunted look in her eyes, however, contrasted sharply with her glamorous appearance. Victoria instinctively knew this woman was Saqib's and Abid's mother.

The eyes of those who have come through times of war and violence carry a look that stays with the person forever. It haunts the eyes of GI's who've seen battle. It haunts those who have witnessed catastrophic events, like 9/11 and Pearl Harbor. It haunts men, women and children who have seen their communities ravaged, watched friends and neighbors slaughtered right outside their doors.

Victoria recognized that look of terror and fear in this woman's eyes; she saw it as easily as she recognized it in herself when she'd look into a mirror.

"Have a good night, Saqib. Abid." Victoria called, raising her hand to wave. The boys looked up from their shoes, gave a half-hearted wave, and continued on their way. Their mother, however, paused and stared at Victoria for a moment. She raised a friendly hand toward the young boys' mother and after a moment, the eyes of the boys' mother softened just a bit. She returned Victoria's wave with a nod. Then she corralled her boys, one in each arm, and guided them out of the courtyard to the waiting car.

⋙⊹⊱⋘

"Victoria, I must speak to you about two of your students. Saqib and Abid." The school's principal sat beside Victoria as she ate her lunch one afternoon with her friend Anum.

"Yes?"

Principal Amira scanned the paperwork she had pinned to a clipboard. "Based on the grades you and other teachers have submitted, these boys have fallen well below our accepted minimum standards. I am going to dismiss them from our institution, and suggest to their parents they enroll them in a government school."

"If I may," Victoria interjected. "I don't believe that these boys suffer from an inability to learn."

"Oh?"

"Their family was forced from Afghanistan and I think the boys are having trouble adjusting emotionally to their new life here. I'm sure if any of us had been displaced to another country due to the war-torn conditions of our own, we would need a good deal of time to adjust as well. Can we offer a special dispensation in this case?"

Principal Amira sighed as she scanned her paperwork once again as if expecting it to provide another answer. "Their grades need to change before the end of the quarter. If there is no improvement, they must leave."

Victoria smiled. "Thank you for your consideration, Amira."

Principal Amira stood up from the table and regarded Victoria with a look that mixed firmness with skepticism. "I trust your judgment in this case." With a curt nod, she spun on her heel and left the room.

"Good job. I wouldn't have had the fortitude to do what you did." Anum gave Victoria a sly smile.

"Those boys deserve another chance." Victoria said a quick prayer to herself, that she could help make the difference the boys from Afghanistan needed to be successful.

That afternoon, Victoria searched the courtyard for the boys' mother. She didn't have to look for long. The tall, beautiful woman was approaching her. She'd left the boys playing by a large Mulberry tree among the small brown leaves and stones that had collected at its base.

"Miss Victoria?" the woman asked, her voice soft and delicate.

"Yes?"

"I am Afroz. Saqib and Abid are my sons."

"What lovely boys you have." Victoria smiled, and hoped the true affection she had for the boys showed. The return smile Afroz offered told Victoria it had.

"The principal told me that the boys' grades are suffering to the point that they could be asked to leave school."

"That's true." Victoria nodded. "If they show improvement before the end of the quarter, that can be avoided."

Afroz smiled again, but the smile did not reach her eyes. None of her smiles did. No true sign of happiness could penetrate the thinly veiled fear that seemed permanently housed there. "We are refugees. The war destroyed everything we had; our home, our business. We were fortunate to make it here alive."

Something from that experience bulldozed its way to the forefront of Afroz's memory, and Victoria sensed she'd gotten lost in her fear.

After a few moments, Afroz could continue. "We were goldsmiths, in business for many years. My husband could save some of our wealth, we moved to Islamabad and opened a shop. It has been a lot for us, to lose everything and rebuild from the ground up. We've tried to keep things normal for the children by sending them to school and encouraging friendships." She paused for a moment, withdrawing into herself, as if she feared she'd said too much. Victoria saw her fear of trusting anyone, even a Christian school teacher.

"My sons told me you were different. They always praise you. Can I ask you to lunch tomorrow, to discuss the boys?" Worry furrowed the mother's brow. Her lips pursed together but there was an eagerness to her posture as she leaned in closer to Victoria. "Please."

The next day was Saturday. Victoria readily accepted Afroz's invitation. They agreed to meet at the school and go to one of Pindi's well known restaurants. As Victoria stood in front of the school, a large black sedan pulled up. The car sparkled, freshly clean, free of the haze and of the dust of the city's streets. Afroz's driver got out of the car and offered Victoria his hand. He opened the door to the back seat and helped her inside. The leather interior smelled new.

"Thank you for meeting with me," Afroz said and grasped Victoria's hand warmly.

"My pleasure," the teacher responded with a smile. The cool breeze from the air conditioner felt good on Victoria's skin, still flushed from standing in the blazing sun with her *chaddar* wrapped around her.

The ride to the restaurant was brief, and the two women engaged in lighthearted discussions about the weather, the beauty of the street vendors' flowers and Pindi's flourishing economics.

When they arrived at their destination, Afroz's driver held out his hand to each woman, helping them from the car. Still somewhat awkward with her *chaddar*, Victoria worked to adjust it properly so as not to drag it behind her. With her sense of style and grace, Afroz did not seem to have the same troubles, and she waited patiently while Victoria arranged her clothing.

As both women ordered masala chai tea, Victoria marveled at the elegant restaurant. While she was growing up, her family was often the wealthiest resident in the neighborhoods where they lived, but Victoria had never eaten in such an opulent, modern restaurant before. The music struck her. Public places often played traditional *Balochi* or *Sindhi* music. Here, they played songs by popular Pakistani artist Junoon, pop tunes by Nazia Hassan, and even a modern remake of a Western disco classic, sung in Urdu.

After a time of tentative silence, Afroz began. "I'd like to tell you a little about our situation, so you can fully understand what is happening with my boys," She took a sip of her tea and Victoria noticed the slight tremor in her hands as she settled the expensive ceramic tea cup back onto the saucer.

"You've told me you were refugees from Afghanistan," Victoria prodded.

Afroz nodded. "During the conflict the boys witnessed atrocities that no child should ever have seen." Afroz's eyes filled with tears. "Women especially, were abused in horrific, unspeakable ways. The boys have become so fearful..."

"I understand what fear can do. I am a Christian woman and these past several years, I've seen more persecution against people of my faith than ever before. It sounds to me that much of what you have experienced in Afghanistan is like what I've experienced here."

"I believe you may be right," Afroz said, tapping a forefinger on her bottom lip, then became silent.

Victoria felt her body stiffen. Suddenly, she doubted the wisdom of revealing that she was Christian. She had hoped that perhaps their journeys, while different, might still on some level be convergent. Had she misread Afroz and thought she was more progressive than she really was? Would this Muslim woman look down on her, as so many others had done once they discovered Victoria was Christian?

Afroz offered Victoria a soft smile. "I desperately want my sons to continue in this school. While they are having difficulty adjusting here, I think a government school would be detrimental to their continued growth. Would you have any interest in tutoring them after school? I would pay you for your time. I am desperate for them to find themselves again and find their place here in Pakistan. Will you help us?"

"Of course I will help you. I am flattered that you would ask."

"The boys have always spoken highly of you. They look at you differently than the other teachers."

"Perhaps through our relative circumstances, we have an understanding between us that others might not."

Afroz smiled. "You may be right about that."

"Will the boys' father have a problem with a Christian woman tutoring your sons in your home?"

"I'm sad you have to ask that question, Victoria, but it's fair." Afroz shook her head. "He's away on business often. Actually, he attended Christian schools; we respect Christians for their contribution to education and to medical fields. Feel free to be open."

"Thank you," Victoria said with a smile.

"You should not be thanking me, my friend. It is I who should thank you."

"In the Bible, the book of Galatians says, 'Carry each other's burdens and in this way you will fulfill the law of Christ.' Helping your boys through their circumstances will also help me with my own. I am grateful for the opportunity you are giving me to become closer to Christ."

Afroz took Victoria's hand. "I am glad we can help one another in matters that are important to both of us."

That day began a productive relationship for all of them. Several days a week for about seven months, Victoria tutored Saqib and Abid in math and computer science, all the subjects that were giving the boys difficulty. With each month of tutoring, their grades improved dramatically.

One afternoon shortly before the quarterly marking period ended, Principal Amira approached Victoria in the staff room.

"It appears your pet students, Saqib and Abid, have improved their work."

"Yes, I've been pleased with their progress in my classes," Victoria responded.

"I'm happy to report that their grades have improved enough for them to remain in school. Should they slip again, however..." Principal Amira let her sentence trail off. The implication that the boys would be asked to leave the school should their grades not remain at their current level was not lost on Victoria.

"Thank you, Principal. I am sure their mother will be thrilled at this good news."

Afroz embraced Victoria that afternoon when she arrived to tutor Saqib and Abid. Both boys, while not comfortable to give her a hug, thanked her time and time again with huge grins spread across their eager faces. For a few moments, the fear that was ever present in their eyes had slipped away, and the boys' genuine personalities peeked through.

"I've done some more research on what the religious persecution of Christians looks like in Pakistan," Afroz said as she poured Victoria a cup of tea. They were seated at the table while the boys completed some written lessons Victoria had given them.

Victoria's eyes grew wide with interest. "What have you learned?"

"I learned enough to know that you and Christians like you don't deserve the treatment you receive just because you believe something differently than the rest of us. I also learned that the persecution you've experienced parallels what we went through in Afghanistan. I'd like to tell you I'm sorry but I know that could never undo anything that's happened to you."

Victoria's eyes filled with tears. "It means more to me than you realize."

"I'll never forgive them," Saqib said. He made no apologies for listening in on his mother's conversation with his teacher. "I hate them."

"Saqib," his mother chastised.

"I will never forgive them. They destroyed our home! They mistreated women in a horrible way in what was our home! How can anyone forgive that?" A hardened look sat sharp as a sword in Saqib's eyes. Victoria could almost see the tendrils of hate flow through his body like a sickness. She'd seen the same in her own eyes years ago, and knew it still boiled just beneath the surface.

"I understand how you feel, Saqib," Victoria said. "I hated those who persecuted me. When I was your age, Muslim children slandered me and called me *paleed*. I had no friends, no one would play with me, just because I was different. I'm guessing you felt that you were alone because you were different too."

"Yes," he admitted and bowed his head.

"That's nothing to be ashamed of. You should never be ashamed of being who you are and for believing the things that you do, even if those ideas are not popular with others around you. Everyone is allowed to have their own beliefs and opinions. What we are not allowed to do is hate because of them." Victoria placed a hand on Saqib's shoulder. "If you hate those who hate you, then you are no better than they are."

"They made my mother cry, they hurt us, they..."

"They did those things, yes," Victoria interrupted. "Because of what they believed. It is always wrong to hurt another person, but the hurt can stop with us if we don't combat that wrongful act with our own form of hatred."

"I can't help it." Saqib's eyes filled with tears. "Other Muslims attacked us. We couldn't understand why they did it. They were filled with hate for us, for no reason."

Victoria looked at the young boy thoughtfully. "I would like to tell you a story about what happened to me." Victoria told him about the time she and her classmates had been run down by the religious protesters. She told him about the fear she felt, the conflict, the anger. "I work every day to repress the hatred and fear I felt."

"How are you able to do that?" Saqib asked.

"My book, the Bible, tells us that 'Hatred stirs up conflict; but love covers over all wrongs.' That is a passage from Proverbs, a book within the Bible that helps to teach us many of life's lessons."

Saqib was thoughtful. "That makes a lot of sense. When I feel hate, it stirs up many feelings of anger and I don't like those feelings. Then, when my mom comes and hugs me and shows me love, I feel better. Is that what your proverb means?"

Victoria smiled and grabbed Saqib for a hug. "That's exactly what it means! Feeling hate will always make us feel badly. Sharing love makes any bad feeling go away."

Later that evening, Victoria feared she may have crossed a line with Afroz and her sons. She was in their proper Muslim home and she dared quote scripture to Afroz's young sons. Victoria had wanted so desperately for them to know that she understood their fear and anger and she hoped by sharing her personal witness would help to allay their feelings. She hoped she hadn't gone too far.

The next afternoon, Victoria watched the children as they were dismissed from the school courtyard. Saqib and Abid no longer hid among the branches of the Mulberry tree. Instead, they were playing a game of soccer with several of their classmates, laughing and shouting, jibing one another just as young boys should do. Victoria saw Afroz standing just out of the boys' view, watching. She turned when she saw Victoria and began walking toward her. Victoria met Afroz halfway.

Tears brimmed in Afroz's deep brown eyes. "Thank you. Look at what your kindness has done for them." She watched as Abid used deft footwork to take the soccer ball from another student.

"Thank you for allowing me to teach them. I may have crossed a line..."

Afroz waved her hand as if swatting a fly. "Our religions may be different, but our lessons are the same. Love and kindness transcend all, don't they? Look how love makes things that were otherwise compromised grow and flourish." The boys spotted their mother and ran to her.

"Have a good night," Victoria called to them. Saqib waved goodbye, a broad smile on his face. Abid raised his hand as if to wave as well, but thought better of it. Instead, he grasped his teacher in a brief, but meaningful, hug.

Victoria knew that she had just completed her first missionary assignment.

CHAPTER 23

"THE CROSS I CANNOT REFUSE"

Victoria was thankful she was making a difference in the lives of her students. The administration was supportive of her innovative approach to teaching, and her commitment to helping students learn. Her Christian faith did not seem to affect her career. She'd finally found a place to grow above the religious prejudice she had suffered.

In her second year of teaching, Victoria had a student in her class, Tanya Hassan, a Muslim girl from an influential and wealthy family. Her computer skills were above those of the other students. Furthermore, Victoria loved Tanya's enthusiasm for learning.

"Miss Victoria, guess where we went on vacation this summer?" Tanya asked one afternoon, bouncing on the balls of her feet.

"It must have been somewhere exciting," Victoria smiled.

"We went to the United States!" Tanya's eyes were bright and her smile wide.

"Oh my, you traveled a long way!"

"My father does business there and while he was meeting with people, my mother and I walked around New York City. Have you ever been there?"

"No, I haven't," Victoria said.

"There were people everywhere. And the buildings were so tall I couldn't see the tops. There were so many cars! You think there's a lot of traffic in Pindi? Ha, it's nothing like New York. The clothes in the shop windows were so... well... my mother made me not look!" Tanya giggled. "I'd love to wear those clothes someday."

Victoria laughed along with her student. Her infectious exuberance was bubbling over and Victoria was easily drawn in.

"Before I forget..." Tanya rooted through her bookbag and pulled out a small black velvet box. "My mother wanted me to give this to you."

Victoria carefully flipped open the box. Inside was a pair of round, sterling silver earrings, with a cross in the center. Victoria gasped.

"Tanya, thank you. I am flattered," Victoria said. She couldn't believe that one of her students would choose a gift for her that spoke of her religion. A gift like this, especially from a Muslim family said to Victoria she was building a bridge between their religions. Inroads were being paved. She was making more of an impact than she had hoped.

Tanya watched as Victoria put on the earrings. Her smile faded.

"How do they look?" Victoria asked, sensing something had changed with her student.

"They are pretty," Tanya said then returned to her desk.

Later that afternoon, Victoria saw Tanya's mother at the courtyard gate. She stood with her arms crossed. Despite the extremism that permeated Pakistan, Mrs. Hassan dared to wear a sleeveless top. Victoria thought perhaps the time she'd spent in America had emboldened her. Maybe she saw in America that people of all religions could live harmoniously; maybe that was what had motivated the generous gift.

"Mrs. Hassan," Victoria called as she approached the daring woman, a smile on her face. "I wanted to thank you for the beautiful gift. Tanya gave them to me this afternoon."

Mrs. Hassan gave Victoria a tight smile in return. "When we were in America this summer, a friend gave them to me. I'm a Muslim, I can't wear them so I thought I'd give them to a Christian."

Victoria was shocked. She tried to maintain a stoic expression, hoping to hide her disappointment. She looked at Tanya who'd walked over to her mother. Tanya's eyes were sad, and she looked down at her feet.

"Thank you," Victoria said, biting back the stern words she wanted to say.

Mrs. Hassan gave Victoria another tight smile, and turned to Tanya. "We should be on our way."

Tanya gave Victoria a small wave and followed her mother to her car. Inside, Victoria seethed.

"This cross you will not accept, I cannot refuse," Victoria muttered to herself. Instead of refusing a gift, Mrs. Hassan decided to accept it, and pass it off to someone else. Victoria felt offended in many ways, mostly, because the bridge she hoped was being built between Christians and Muslims now seemed to have been destroyed. Just when she thought she'd seen progress, and prepared to step foot onto that proverbial bridge, it had disappeared.

Later that year, Victoria received word she had been promoted, and would move to another school. She would never take the job.

Ishaq, her father, had become seriously ill. Victoria knew her father was biding his time, waiting for when Jesus to call him home. She stayed close to him; she held his hand and wiped the perspiration from his brow. Now, he slept most of the time; occasionally he had moments of clarity. As his condition worsened, those moments were fewer and farther between.

Victoria encouraged her father to drink, but he refused everything. She sat with her father day and night; pain racked his body, and he continued to waste away before her eyes. Many times, she found herself pressing her hand to his heart, to make sure it was still beating.

One evening, Victoria clasped her father's frail, cold hand within both of hers and whispered prayers. "Oh father," she murmured. "How I wish I could take this cross from you just as Jesus's disciples tried to as he was being led to his death. I wish I could somehow intercede and ease your suffering."

Her father's eyes snapped open, and a gentle smile crossed his dry, cracked lips.

"There she is, Victoria. Do you see her?" He managed to lift his head, and looked towards the foot of the bed.

Victoria looked but saw nothing. "I don't see anyone Papa."

"She's beautiful."

"Who Papa?"

"Your mother. She's come to take me home." With that, Ishaq's hand went limp in hers and his eyes closed once again. He took one great breath in and out and went forever silent.

A waxy pallor covered his face, and Victoria knew her father had gone to join her mother in the Kingdom of Jesus. Great sobs racked her body as Victoria cradled her father's lifeless body.

A man of kindness, forgiveness and patience had gone to Heaven. He left behind a penitent daughter, someone to carry on his lessons, as his father had done before him. Talib and Ishaq lived on within Victoria, and she would ensure their message endured. She would take the cross they had carried.

CHAPTER 24

"AN UNKNOWN BROTHER"

After mourning her father, Victoria knew that to remain within her family home she would need a new job. Fortunately, she found one in short order.

Victoria provided administrative support for two Muslim men, Fazal and Masood. At first, her stomach did somersaults whenever the two men entered the office. Victoria averted her eyes from them, knowing some Muslim men became angry if a woman looked straight at them, especially a Christian woman. Their distaste for Christians could affect her entire family. Victoria did her best to stifle her fears, and tempered her boldness. She hoped to maintain peace in her work environment. She need not have worried.

The very first morning, Fazal greeted his new assistant with a smile.

"Good Morning my sister," he said. Victoria was unable to keep the surprise from her face and she was more than pleased when Fazal continued his friendly greetings each morning.

All her life Victoria had convinced herself that because all Muslims followed the same book and teachings, they all acted the same, and treated Christians poorly. Fazal and Masood proved her wrong; they showed that her prejudice was part of the problem.

She bit her lip as she thought about some of the times she assumed she was rejected because of her faith; maybe she was the one prejudging.

Both men had better values than many other people Victoria knew, Muslim or Christian. They were considerate, thoughtful and above all, they treated Victoria, a Christian woman, with kindness and respect; most Muslim men did not. After a while, the men and their Christian administrative assistant built a bridge of understanding between them, a bridge that fostered a lasting friendship.

"Victoria, why are you working here?" Fazal asked her one afternoon when business was slow.

"Both my parents have passed away. I need this job in to be able to maintain the house where I live. I also have a wandering mind, so it was to help me to behave," Victoria smirked. Fazal laughed.

"You are a bright woman. You have a degree, don't you?"

"Yes, in math and computer sciences."

"Then why are you here? Go back to school; be a college professor. Don't get stuck in a government office with a bunch of men who will do nothing but disrespect you for being a woman."

Fazal was a devout Muslim who never missed prayer time. He belonged to a good, financially sound Muslim family, yet he said things to Victoria that seemed uncharacteristic of other Muslims she knew.

One afternoon, she overheard parts of a heated conversation between Fazal and another office employee.

"... that *Christian woman* in your office," a man said. His voice dripped with contempt.

"You have no cause to speak of her in such a demeaning tone," Fazal retorted. "You've never spoken to her, you know nothing about her, yet somehow you feel it's ok to speak ill of her?"

"She is beneath you."

"She is a colleague, employed here because she has something valuable to contribute. She deserves the same respect we all do."

Fazal stormed back into his office, slamming the door behind him. Victoria had never seen his dark eyes flash with so much anger before.

Victoria waited for Fazal to calm down, then she knocked on his office door. He sheepishly invited her to come in. Then the young Christian woman spoke in her own defense, confident he would listen.

"There is no need to fight my battles for me, Fazal. At this point in my life, I am a well-seasoned soldier, and, I've found many are simply not worth fighting."

Fazal wiped a hand down his face and shook his head.

"My sister, I am sorry you had to hear that. Some people will never learn to look beyond the lines of division we place upon ourselves. They are too narrow-minded. Divisions are easy. When people classify others by their skin color, their religion or their economic status, they just reinforce stereotypes. That is the thinking of the ignorant. I apologize to you that so many of my Muslim brethren adhere to that way of thinking. They embrace the division and ignore the individual."

Victoria smiled. If only all people could subscribe to Fazal's way of thinking, the world could find itself at peace.

The next day, Fazal brought Victoria a gift. It was a beautiful black printed *chaddar*. He said to her, "Sister, allow me to wrap this around you." Victoria allowed it, comforted by the sibling-like relationship that had evolved between them.

As a Christian, Victoria chose not to cover her head in Islamabad. The progressive climate in the city allowed her to keep her head uncovered without repercussions. But she understood the point of Fazal's gift. He cared about her as much as he would his own sister, and he wanted to spare her the disrespect of some of the Muslim men in the office. Wearing the chaddar would show the men that she respected their religion enough to cover her head, as was their custom, and thus invite them to show her respect as well.

Her friendship with Fazal made it clear not all Muslims were like those who brutally beat Christians, and left them for dead in the streets, or spat at those who were lower caste. There were Muslims who were full of love, kindness and who respected everyone around them. They didn't use their religion to laud power over those who did not believe, rather they sought to learn from them and embrace those differences. Victoria wondered where these Muslims had been all her life? The more she thought about this, the more she believed God was teaching her a lesson. She had tried to command respect all her life, but maybe to get respect, she had to start by respecting others.

Through Fazal, she'd learned to respect Muslims, a goal she had tried to achieve for so, so long a time. This was a true milestone; another seed of her faith mission was growing to fruition. It was possible to forage a kinship among Muslim men and women. She would find that same respect in another Muslim, a woman.

CHAPTER 25

"THE LOST SHEEP"

While Victoria found an unexpected kinship with the Muslim men at her office, she found herself an outcast among some of the congregants at her church. After all the attempts at making a good life with the Christian man her uncle had found for her, the relationship had failed.

Her church, which had always been her foundation, now treated her as if she were no longer a part of their community. Feelings of guilt haunted her; she had been rejected by the community she'd come to rely on. She had trouble sleeping, and wandered around her home at night, praying her life would take a turn for the better.

One afternoon, her co-worker, Saima, approached Victoria with an invitation. "Come with me, tonight. My sister is hosting a prayer meeting."

"You are Muslim..."

"And you are Christian. That doesn't matter." Saima patted Victoria's shoulder. "You need help and support and you will find it with these women."

Reluctantly, Victoria agreed. It was the first time she'd given in to an attempt from the Muslim community to evangelize her. Deep within, Victoria felt ashamed. She needed a sense of community, a sense of forgiveness, so she convinced herself to go.

By going, Victoria believed she could assuage some of the guilt she felt for the prejudice she had harbored against Muslims. With so many negative feelings pressing on her, Victoria hoped that at least one piece of guilt could be lifted.

Rabia, the leader of the Muslim women's study group, approached Victoria after the meeting. "Victoria, you've been a wonderful addition to our group."

"Thank you." Victoria looked at her feet unsure how to accept the compliment.

"When Saima told us a Christian woman was coming to our group, I'll admit, I was shocked. When I found out how well you know the *Quran*, I was impressed."

"You're kind," Victoria said, squeezing the hand Rabia offered her.

"Having a woman with your level of learning about Islam is a powerful affirmation to many of the women. Why are you no longer with your church?"

"It is a personal matter; one I prefer not to discuss." Victoria did not want to give the kind Muslim woman some reason to reject her.

Rabia put her arm around Victoria. Surprised, she found this small effort was the most comfort she'd had from another person since Fazal had helped her with her *chaddar*. Then Rabia said, "My sister, we will help you through this. I promise."

Victoria went back to the Muslim prayer meeting the following week. Rabia said,

"This evening, I would like to ask sister Victoria to read aloud from the *Quran*."

Victoria, used to reading from the *Quran* from when she was in school, read the selected passage. Within the large passage from Surat An-Nisa was this: 'It may well be that Allah will pardon them. Allah is Ever Pardoning, Ever Forgiving.'

At home, later that evening, Victoria was restless. She paced the small home for hours. How she craved the easy forgiveness given by Allah and the Muslim women. She snatched her Bible, forgotten on her bookshelf, and began to read. She was determined to search for peace and a renewed faith from God's Word. After reading several pages, Victoria fell to her knees.

"God, please, leave your flock and come after me. I have strayed, and I need you to show me how to find peace and how to overcome this guilt I live with. Where can I find peace? What is next for me?"

She slept that night with the Bible next to her, a sleep that was more restful than it had been in months. In the morning, she opened the book and read a passage from Scripture; "Come to me all who are weary and heavy laden, and I will give you rest." Victoria felt confident that Jesus had sent His Holy Spirit to comfort her.

Now she knew that something wonderful was coming for her, she just had to make sure to keep her eyes open to recognize it. The miracle she was looking for did not take long to arrive.

CHAPTER 26
"THE STRENGTH TO FORGIVE"

A hesitant knock at the front door interrupted Victoria from the book she was reading. She was not expecting anyone, but thinking it was some sort of emergency, she quickly rushed to the door. When she opened it, she sucked in deep breath, and fury caught in her chest.

He was much taller and broader than she'd remembered, now several years older, but his almond shaped eyes and aquiline nose remained the same as they'd been when he was a child.

"William." Victoria crossed her arms in front of her, heat roiling up the back of her neck and flushing her cheeks.

"You remembered," he said, with a twisted smile.

Victoria went mute. She wanted to punch him, kick him, scream at him, just like she would have done to anyone who had rejected her. At the same time, she wanted to grab him in a tight embrace and hold him forever.

Finally she blurted out, "Why are you here?" What could they possibly have to say to one another that was going to change anything now?

"I came to humbly beg your parents' forgiveness.

Victoria narrowed her eyes at him. "Well, it's too late for that. They passed away years ago. My mother, consumed with grief because of what you did and my father a few years later."

"I..." he started, but could not finish his thought. Tears had welled up in his eyes; Victoria knew the news she'd shared had hit him hard. "I'm sorry Victoria," he finally managed. Can I come in and explain? I want to apologize for all the hurt I caused you and your family.

Victoria steadied herself, and silently prayed. She then moved aside from the doorway and waved a hand. "Come in," she offered. "We have a lot to talk about. I will make tea."

"Thank you," he said softly and walked inside. "Your kindness to invite me in is beyond what I deserve."

Victoria said nothing in reply. The duo remained in silence while Victoria busied herself in the kitchen making chai tea for both of them. Her emotions were twisting and swirling within her like a tornado, growing in their power without an outlet. How dare he think he could come here and expect an apology could erase the years of pain his decision had caused – not just for her, but for her dear mother and father?

She returned to the dining area and placed a cup of tea in front of him. He gave her a grateful smile. The smile reminded Victoria of this man's easygoing demeanor, his charm, his grace, his acceptance of everyone around him. She remembered the warmth and compassion that had ingratiated him to everyone who met him.

William had been popular with the village men, with whom he would have endless conversations about business or politics. And when the children of the village saw him, they'd rush to his side, knowing he would play cricket with them. Where had that man been when he'd broken their engagement? Which man was seated before her now? She sat and just stared at him.

After taking a long sip of his tea, William softly said, "I wasn't expecting to see you here, at your parents' house."

"I could say the same."

William chuckled. "I am glad to see you haven't lost your spirit."

"What do you know about what I've lost?" Emboldened, Victoria continued. "You made a decision that I've had to live with, while you carried on with your charmed life, traveling around the world."

"I regret what that decision did to you, but I don't regret making it. I would do it all again."

"You think so little of me? That you could cast me off on some whim?"

"No, not at all!" William's eyes opened wide in surprise. "It wasn't a whim. I did it for you."

"Oh really?"

"Victoria, you were a child of fourteen!"

"An acceptable marrying age. I may have been immature..."

"It had nothing to do with maturity," William interrupted. "I have spent time in other parts of the world and I saw that fourteen is entirely too young to marry. At fourteen, you are still a child, still growing and developing. To marry anyone at that age, to me, seemed immoral then, and it still does now."

"You could have promised my parents that you would come back in five years." Victoria kept on talking, her eyes down, tears beginning to come. For years she had endured too much shame and anger. Her mother carried her hurt to her grave. Her father was insulted, shamed in front of his brothers and sisters.

William looked away. In a soft voice, he said, "I was twenty-two years old at the time. I should have known how much trouble I would cause. Please forgive me."

Victoria sat back in her chair, studying his face, and staring at William, in silence. His eyes seemed to plead with her to understand his decision. It was hard for her accept, but the harder she thought about it, the more she believed that with time she might be able to understand.

Victoria had recently become involved with a progressive women's group, a human rights organization. She had learned much about the plight of women and children throughout the world, but especially in the Middle East. Certain cultural norms that she'd always accepted without question were exposed through this organization. These revelations had caused Victoria to look at some customs more closely and their impact on those who suffered repercussions from them. The idea of a 'child-bride', a custom widely practiced in Pakistan, was one of them.

"As an adult woman who has become educated, I can respect your decision and admire that even at such a young age, you thought that way. It is a progressive way of thinking."

"I am overwhelmed by your generosity...."

"But," Victoria interrupted and stuck a pointer finger in the air to command attention as she used to do in her classroom. "I still have a hard time accepting the repercussions on my life. I am angry with you, William. I spent a lot of my life being rejected by Muslims simply because I was a Christian. Then I suffer what is one of the most offensive slights at your hands. Of all people on this earth, I never would have expected you to turn me away so suddenly, despite how stalwart your motivations may have been."

"I admit, I did not handle things as well as I should have. It was abrupt and terse. Had I been soft about it, I would have been persuaded to compromise my principals. Had I seen you, I know I would have relented." William sighed and ran his hands down his face. "My father all but stopped talking to me. It's taken years for us to repair our relationship. It wasn't until I promised to come here today to make amends with your family that he accepted me as his son again."

"I am sorry to hear that. Your father, from what I recall, has always been a kind man." Victoria felt herself softening toward William, almost against her will. Could a few honest moments erase years of misunderstanding?

"A stubborn man, too." This remark caused Victoria to chuckle and she felt her heart soften even more.

"What do you think your father would have said to me today?" William asked. "Showing up unannounced on your doorstep begging for forgiveness?"

Victoria smiled. "Before or after he insulted you harshly enough to make even the most hardened criminal cry?"

William burst out in laughter and Victoria joined in. "Fair enough," he said. Then his eyes grew serious. He went to reach for Victoria's hand but she pulled it back. To touch her, even in the most benign of ways, would cross the boundary she'd unknowingly set for herself. "I've missed you, Victoria. Please know that nothing I did was your fault. Even though you, no doubt, felt that way."

"I did. Every single day since you broke our engagement."

"I know. I am so sorry. Is there any way you can forgive me?"

Victoria raised her eyes heavenward and gave a short, sarcastic, bark of laughter. "What makes you think you deserve it?"

"A wise man once told me that once you know Jesus, it is not hard to convert your heart. I know how close you are with Jesus and how he guides you through your life. Perhaps you will find it within yourself to ask him to guide you on a path of forgiveness."

Victoria knew he spoke the truth, she'd heard it from her grandfather as well. Victoria did know Jesus, she always had, it was just she felt that sometimes He presented her with such formidable challenges, she didn't know how to face them without stumbling. And now he'd given her yet another to face.

"I don't know how to forgive you," she answered him honestly. "But I can try."

"I can expect nothing more from you. Thank you."

<hr />

After William left that afternoon, Victoria's emotions, both positive and negative, cycled through her and left her in a perpetual state of self-doubt. Would she tarnish the memory of her mother and father if she were to forgive him? William, the man who aided in the death of her parents? Would she leave a scar on her heart if she chose not to forgive him? She was being given the opportunity to ease some of the pain that she felt, the anger, the bitterness and distrust she'd felt toward him by allowing herself to forgive him. Could she allow herself to forgive and accept letting go of the negativity she'd harbored within for so long?

Then she considered her faith mission and she fell to her knees in prayer.

"Lord Jesus. I've committed myself to working to forgive Muslims for their transgressions toward me. I've worked hard to offer the love and friendship to Muslims that comes from the gift of forgiveness. I've often found it difficult to do so. Can it be because I've not learned to forgive William? If I offer him forgiveness, can I then more productively fulfill my faith mission?"

It seemed that having a mature, educated man at her side would go a long way to helping her serve poor Christian children, children like her, who felt like outcasts in their society.

These thoughts lingered with Victoria and she ruminated on them throughout the next several days. Then she received a letter:

"My dearest Victoria,

Words cannot express how my heart leapt when I saw your beautiful face. I am not sure what I expected when I came to your home to beg for forgiveness, but when you responded to me with honesty and integrity, I was reminded of how much I loved you years ago, and how much I still do.

If you can find it in your heart to forgive me, I would be eternally grateful. I understand that it might take some time, but I am committed to giving you all the time you want or need to do so.

I want to take you away from this conflicted life here in Pakistan. I want to care for you and take you away from any dangers you may face here. I promise to always love and protect you from this day forward, if you will allow it.

All my love,
William."

After much prayer and soul searching, Victoria discovered she could forgive William for hurting her all those years ago. She had found the courage to forgive him, the faith to carry it through and the ability to stand up for herself. God had awakened within her a gift; He strengthened her with the Holy Spirit to use her voice to speak up for herself, to speak out against injustices and to offer forgiveness and compassion to others. Her faith had given her a new voice and it was achieved through unconditional forgiveness. Along with that forgiveness, Victoria found something unexpected had happened; she'd fallen in love with William all over again.

In an intimate ceremony, Victoria and William married to the joy of their families. Their marriage solidified, their union perfect, they looked forward to the next stage in their lives.

CHAPTER 27

"INDEPENDENCE DAY"

O n May 11,1993, eleven-year-old Salmat Masih, from a village near Lahore, was accused of writing blasphemous remarks on the walls of a mosque. According to the Los Angeles Times, the boy was beaten, and forced to implicate his father, Rehmat, and uncle, Manzoor. The writing on the mosque walls was Arabic. Everyone in their village knew Salmat and Manzoor were illiterate, and could not possibly have written anything, especially in Arabic. Even so, they were put in jail.

The three were released on bail. When they showed up for a hearing, an angry mob broke out; villagers intended to take justice into their own hands. The three accused ran for their lives, pursued by a growing, howling crowd.

Militia from the nearby police fought through the crowd, trying to save the three accused. Just in time, they rescued the men, and struggled to bring them to safety within the embassy, but gunshots from the crowd rang out. People ducked for cover amid shouts and screams. Members of the mob fled in different directions. In the center lay Manzoor Masih, dead, in a pool of his own blood.

Victoria could sit back no longer. Her anger flared to a point it could not be satisfied. She joined many other Christian human rights activists who worked to get help for the victims of the Lahore attack. The two survivors were brought to a Christian-run facility, much like a boarding house. While there, Victoria had a chance to speak with the eleven-year-old.

He did not speak a word, he was merely cowering on the chair, his almond shaped eyes staring into a void. Victoria knew that it would be hard to break through that fear. Victoria assumed the boy was going over in his mind how he had been pursued by people who wanted to beat him, and kill him; he had been hunted like an animal. He relived watching his brother gunned down before his very eyes. There was no longer room within him to be the little boy he was before this incident. There was no compassion, no love, no joy left within this child. His eyes revealed to Victoria what remained of that boy, fear. For now. That fear would grow and it would change and it would become the ugliest, the most rooted form of hate there was and the idea of it broke Victoria's heart.

With the aid of European diplomats, the young boy and his father were sent to Germany as refugees. While Victoria was grateful they'd survived, and been given aid, she grew more frustrated and angry at those within her own country who oppressed Christians with such hostility. The anger within her toward the Muslim leaders of her country who allowed the rights of Christians to be so blatantly violated incited the deep-rooted anger within her that she had pushed down for years but could ignore no longer.

"I cannot watch this happen any longer!" Victoria cried one evening and she threw the newspaper she was reading to the ground. "How can any mother stand by and allow this to continue? What is becoming of Pakistan? It is now so influenced by Islamic Law that true justice no longer exists!"

William picked up the paper from the floor and scanned the headlines. A protest had broken out. Young Christians marched to protest the death of the Christian man who'd been accused, but not convicted, of blasphemy.

"My wife, I understand your frustration. The treatment these people have endured is unacceptable."

"We must do something. I will get together some Christian human rights supporters. We can work together, we will figure it out."

A few days later, William departed for another long journey to the United States. He was conducting more and more business there and he was out of the country for extensive periods of time. Victoria's brother, Sameer and his family came over for dinner to keep her company and help with the household duties while William was away. The children played together in the courtyard while the adults enjoyed their after-dinner chai tea.

"Some *Marzais* have joined with us to protest."

The *Marzais* are an Islamic group also known as *Qadiyani* Muslims. They are another sect of the Islamic religion who believe in a prophet after the Prophet Mohammed. Traditional Muslims think very little of this sect. It is said that they'd save the life of a Christian before a *Marzai*.

Sameer sighed. "Victoria, all you can talk about is this women's movement. What do you really think you'll be able to accomplish?"

"We intend to fight Sharia law and all of the injustices it brings!"

"Hasn't the law declared Marzais to be non-Muslims? What clout does that bring to your little group?"

"If they didn't do that, they would be considered blasphemers and could get killed," Victoria said. "Extremism cannot be tolerated and the Marzais see this."

"Very little can be accomplished, and for what? All you are doing is opening yourself and your family up to be targets."

"You'd rather watch others suffer while you sit idly by?"

"You put everyone at risk with your open hostility toward the Muslim oppressors."

"And what is your plan to do God's work, Sameer? Have you thought about what you are going to do to change this world so that your children won't have to suffer as we did?"

"Father was always right about you. He said you'd never change and you haven't. You are still that angry, hateful kid who didn't care about how much you could hurt your family. All you care about is opening your mouth and speaking your mind. You do not care that you could hurt those around you." Sameer threw his napkin to the ground. "I don't need my family to suffer for your foolishness."

"You're the fool, Sameer."

"Stay away from me, Victoria. From our sisters, too. You are a bad influence for the girls in our family. Your Western, liberal ideas are unacceptable to us. Stay away, from my daughters and my wife as well. I do not want them to follow your example."

Sameer headed for the door. Just before he reached it, he spun around and glared at his sister, his eyes ablaze with fury. "Don't tell anyone you know me, Victoria. It's the least you could do while you're on this suicide mission."

Victoria shook as Sameer slammed the door behind him. She knew this time she'd gone too far. She had wanted her children to grow up surrounded with the love of their aunts, uncles and cousins. Her altercation with Sameer would prevent that. How long it would take for a reconciliation she did not know. Such deeply ingrained fear could prolong their rift forever if they'd let it.

⊷╬╬⊶

"Victoria, we must talk," William said, his eyes burdened with something she knew was going to be difficult for her to handle.

"You can tell me anything, William," Victoria said softly, but still her stomach roiled with nausea. She already knew that whatever William was about to tell her would have significant consequences to their current way of life.

He took her hands in his gently. "As you know, I've been spending a lot of time in the United States for my job."

Victoria nodded. Since the new year, he'd been gone for weeks on end. It was as if he were living in the United States and only visiting his family in Pakistan. It was beginning to put a strain on their relationship.

"You and the children will need to move there, permanently. I want you and our sons to join me."

Victoria felt lightheaded. The United States? She'd never ventured out of Pakistan before and now William wanted to move everyone to a foreign country where they didn't know the culture. She had become successful standing up for the rights of so many oppressed women and children. How could she leave them now?

"We would move to Florida. It's beautiful there. The climate is warm just like here. Palm trees are everywhere! This land is opulent, all the homes are big and beautiful. I know you will love it there."

Victoria shook her head. "This is a lot for me to comprehend right now."

"I understand, I do, and I think it's best." William lifted Victoria's chin so he would be able to look her in the eyes. "You are withering here, Victoria. You are angry and always feeling persecuted. It's not like that in America. Everyone from many different cultures is welcome in America." Victoria shook her head, unsure. "I promise, we will make a good life there. One where you won't be burdened by these terrible feelings."

So, it was decided. William and Victoria would raise their family and live their faith in a new land, a land where they would not have to be afraid, where they would not be prejudged, or insulted because of how they dressed, or what religion they practiced.

⊷⊷ ⊶⊷

Victoria and their sons, Adam and Thomas, had been in the United States for less than a week. Between recovering from the long plane ride, sleeping off the jet lag and the pressure to get their house in order after their move, William decided to take everyone to the local Florida beach to see the Independence Day fireworks. More impressive than the beautiful display of lights was the experience Victoria had that day. People from all races, all cultures were gathered together under God's magnificent evening sky to celebrate the birth of this great nation. Together. This culture didn't seem to divide based on religious preferences. Religion wasn't law here. This gave everyone the freedom to celebrate together, without prejudice.

Soon after the Independence Day celebration, Victoria felt a strong draw to attend church. She joined a local church and found the clergy and administrative staff warm and welcoming. Inside she noticed this church had national flags hung about, representing the multi-cultural base of their congregation. The fact that this church embraced the cultural mix of their congregants made Victoria feel even more welcome. Soon she began working in the nursery during one service per week to help her church community and integrate herself and her family into this new Christian community.

The first year in the United States was like paradise. William's business was going well; economically their family was not struggling. They fit in well with their neighbors and were embraced and welcomed by their church community. Life had changed for Victoria and she finally felt free enough to let go of the anger she'd harbored for so long.

Then came September 11, 2001.

CHAPTER 28

"JUDGMENT"

It was a beautiful morning in Naples, Florida; the sky a crystalline blue, the late summer breeze a refreshing contrast to the humidity they'd endured recently. When Victoria heard the news, she reacted with horror.

At first, she thought this was some sort of stunt, a cruel trick. The fact that such a heinous act had happened on American soil was unfathomable. When the school called, asking that she pick up her children, and when Victoria's government office closed for the safety of its employees, Victoria knew the attack on Manhattan was real.

A radical fundamentalist Muslim sect had wrought acts of terror on American soil. Just when she thought she'd been freed of them, they came here. The unrelenting fear that she'd learned to keep in check came roiling back up.

"Is it true, Mom?" Thomas asked when Victoria had made sure he and Adam were safely secured in the car. "Did terrorists attack the United States?"

"We don't know all of the details yet," Victoria said, trying to deflect the conversation to protect her boys. She didn't know what to tell them, how to approach what had happened today with them. She'd prayed she'd never need to talk to them about anything like this, especially not now that they'd moved to the United States.

That night, Victoria prayed for the knowledge of how to talk to her children about terrorism. When she'd lived in Pakistan, she'd had to fight to remain a loving Christian, despite the hateful looks that would be cast her way. Now, because people that looked like her had caused such devastation, throwing her new country into a state of fear, Victoria was receiving those same, hateful looks in her adopted country. She felt as if she was no longer accepted by the communities that had welcomed her.

The next day, Adam got in the car after school, downtrodden.

"What is wrong?" Victoria asked.

After some hesitation, Adam opened up.

"There is a Pakistani boy in our class. He doesn't speak much English, so sometimes I translate for him, to help him. Now that the kids in our class know that fundamentalist Muslims killed all those people, the kids at school are mean to him; they call him names. I try to stick up for him, but I'm just one person. It's not fair - he's really scared."

"And today an American boy in my class asked me if I was Muslim," Adam said sadly. "I told him I was Christian."

Victoria's heart broke for that child who, though uninvolved, was being blamed for a terrible attack, only because of his looks and his religion. As the empathy for this child grew, Victoria recognized that something incredible had just happened to her. For the first time in her life, Victoria found compassion for a Muslim.

When Adam asked if the boy could come to their house to play, his mother readily agreed. She went to pick up the young boy at his home. Both of his parents met Victoria outside. With a great smile, Victoria exited her vehicle and smoothed down the front of her sundress. She was taken aback by a look of derision from the child's father.

"I am pleased to meet you," Victoria said, a bright smile on her face. "What part of Pakistan are you from?"

The boy's father hesitated for a bit, his eyes taking Victoria in and growing angrier. "A village about thirty miles outside of Pindi."

"Oh, I used to work at a school in Rawalpindi-Islamabad."

"How long have you been in the United States?" the father demanded, ignoring Victoria's attempt at making a familiar connection between them.

"About a year now," Victoria smiled.

"Then you should know where the local mosque is."

"I know there is a mosque, but we don't go there. We are a Christian family."

"No wonder you are dressed like a Western woman. A Muslim woman would never be seen in such a state."

Victoria cast a glance at the boy's mother, fully covered in traditional Muslim dress. She didn't try to speak a word. Victoria wasn't sure if she was kept from speaking, or simply didn't know English.

"Boy, time to get inside," the father bellowed in Urdu. Without a second thought, the young man sprang from the ground where he was sitting with Adam and ran to their home. Without a further word to Victoria, the boy's father and mother went into their home.

Victoria and Adam were left standing on their walkway. Adam stood motionless, trying to understand what just happened. The boy he had befriended was not coming home with him.

Victoria became angry. Muslims still wanted to keep a distance from her, even here, because she was Christian.

Adam and the little boy played together, at school. Several times Victoria bumped into the boy's father at school pick up. Each time he mostly kept to himself, although at times did try to make pleasant conversation. Victoria wanted to forget what had happened, to put it behind her and her son, but found she could not. That old anger began to creep into her heart.

"Adam, what has you so sad?" Victoria asked one afternoon as her son got into the car. He looked quite forlorn."

"My friend from Pakistan moved away."

"Oh dear, that seems sudden. You both loved to play together, I am sure you are sad about it. Didn't they just move to Florida not long ago?"

"I thought so. He said his parents bought a gas station in New Jersey, so they are moving there tomorrow."

That evening, and for many subsequent evenings, Victoria spent time thinking about that child. Was he ever accepted by his peers? How was he handling his new school? Was he able to make friends or were other students unable to see beyond the fact that he was Muslim? Those childhood feelings Victoria suffered of rejection resurfaced. When would they ever stop? Maybe they wouldn't, not for the boy, not for her.

⋙ ⋘

Between Thanksgiving and Christmas in 2001, Victoria and William decided to take in a movie at the Hollywood Theater near their home. It was chilly that day, cooler than what people in Southwest Florida were accustomed to. The only thing in her closet that she had that would weather the cold spell was her traditional Pakistani clothing.

William was getting tickets for the show while Victoria waited in the movie lobby. She looked around and saw a group of teenagers, laden with tattoos and piercings, idling nearby. They were close enough to her that she couldn't help overhearing what they were saying:

"Look at her dress," Victoria overheard one of the girls exclaim. "She's so beautiful!" Victoria felt a blush creep up on her cheeks. It was a high compliment.

"Yeah, but you never know what she might be hiding under that dress," one of the teen boys commented, a sly smile crossing his face." That familiar feeling of anger gnawed at Victoria.

"What do you mean by that?" she heard the girl say, challenging her friend.

"There could be a bomb under there!" The boy balled one hand in a fist, then quickly released it, making the sound of a bomb exploding. The group began to laugh, stealing glances Victoria's way. She wanted to speak up, she wanted to tell them that they were wrong and their jokes and judgments were harsh, cruel and untrue.

"That's wrong on all kinds of levels," the teen girl remarked, as she and the rest of her group left to go into the theater.

"Ready?" William smiled at Victoria. Victoria forced a steely smile and settled into her seat but she remained uncomfortable throughout the movie because of her clothing. Her focus was more about what had happened that afternoon, rather than the film.

She likened the American Christian teenagers to the Muslims in Pakistan. Where in Pakistan it was religion that divided them, here in the United States it was the differences in how people look that creates the divide. Her mission, she knew now more than ever, was to help people of all faiths see each other as created in God's image and loved by Him. That is how she wanted to spend the rest of her life.

❧ ❧

Victoria's church had decided to celebrate Christmas this year with an International Foods Day.

Victoria was excited about sharing her Pakistani cuisine with her new friends at church, and, of course, sampling the foods of other countries. This was a chance to celebrate the cultural diversity that existed within the congregation. God willing, this would create greater appreciation for different cultures. This was exactly what Victoria saw more and more as her calling. She needed time off from her new job to help set cook for the dinner and help to set things up.

She approached her supervisor, Henry, at the clerk's office where she now worked, and requested the day off.

Henry's eyebrows furrowed. "Why do you need time off at Christmas? We try to reserve time off around the holidays for the Christians who celebrate them."

Victoria crossed her arms. "How do you know I'm not Christian?" she demanded.

"Well, you're from Pakistan, right?"

And there it was, again. People made assumptions about Victoria because of her outward appearance instead of getting to know her. Because she was from the Middle East, it was automatically assumed she was Muslim. "I'm Christian. You didn't bother to learn that about me, though."

"I'm sorry, Victoria, I didn't know," Henry said, chagrined. "Anyway, I can't give you the day off."

"Because I'm Pakistani?"

"No. We don't have enough coverage during the holidays because of all the others to whom I have already given the day off."

"You didn't know I would need time off because you assumed something about me that wasn't true."

"I'm sorry, Victoria." Henry turned and walked back into his office, leaving Victoria standing there, seething.

Victoria knew more and more she had to do something, something that would help others see the person, and not just their outward appearance.

⊨╬ ╬⊨

One of the places Victoria and William's family found acceptance was at their church. Although they were the only family from a Muslim country, they found most of the people to be kind.

One morning, though, Victoria was volunteering in the church nursery, helping to take care of babies and toddlers so their parents could worship in peace. She had done this every week for the past year. A new mother brought her recently baptized baby into the nursery. She handed the infant to Daisy, her partner in the nursery, and whispered loud enough for Victoria to hear, "Don't you let that woman touch my baby."

The mother cast an ugly glare at Victoria who was working with a couple of the pre-school aged children. Victoria's eyes filled with tears. It took everything she had not to allow them to spill down her cheeks.

"Your child will be fine in my care or Victoria's care," Daisy said. She walked to Victoria and put her arm around her.

Shaking, Victoria said, "No harm will come to your child here."

The mother's mouth opened as if to speak, but nothing came out. The young woman had not expected the nursery volunteer she insulted to be able to speak English. After a muttered excuse, the mother went back into the church to worship.

"I'm so sorry, Victoria," Daisy said. "Some people just aren't accepting of those from your country. Especially now. I'm sure you can understand that."

All Victoria understood was that with one brief encounter, she had been the object of prejudice, and she resented it. She could not sit by and allow the anger that simmered among some of the members at her church to go unaddressed. Victoria proposed to the Pastor that she speak to those who were interested during their Wednesday evening Bible study class.

When Victoria arrived, she was thrilled to see that the participants had nearly doubled. Clearly, the fact that the church would be addressing this issue had impacted many congregants. Victoria, purposely dressed in traditional Pakistani clothing, straightened her back and addressed her fellow congregants.

"Good evening, thank you all for coming. I am Victoria, a fellow member of this church, what's more, a Christian, a Pakistani Christian. We are here this evening to discuss the tragic events of 9-11 and how to handle our fears.

"It's important to know that even though a group of radicalized Muslims committed these atrocities, these people are not representative of all Muslims. There are many good, kind Muslims. It's like saying that Jeffrey Dahmer, a serial killer, was Christian, therefore all Christians are serial killers. We know that is not true. You may not want to hear this, or believe it, but I am telling you not all Muslims are terrorists."

Victoria talked about Fazal and Masood, the gentlemen who treated her like a sister when she worked at her government job. She spoke of her grandfather, and his conversion. "Could I have hated my kind, loving grandfather when he was Muslim, but loved him when he's Christian? What hypocrisy that would be!"

Victoria further explained her grandfather's moving story. "He always loved his parents and his brothers and sisters, even when they shunned him. Am I supposed to not love my Muslim relatives because of their religion? Of course not."

The reaction was swift. Many that night expressed their concern over their safety, and that of their families. They feared more attacks would come. They didn't know which Muslims they could trust. The radicals who took down the Twin Towers had done their work well. Nine Eleven was not just about taking down two buildings; it was about tearing apart the American quilt of diverse ethnic groups. They had gotten Americans to fear, even hate, each other.

Victoria continued her impassioned talk: "We are all like book covers. The outside cover tells us a minimal amount of information, enough to interest us to read more or enough to tell us not to bother, and put the book back down.

If you don't take the chance to read the book, you'll never know what you might have missed. That is why I wore my Pakistani clothing. If you were to look at me tonight, outside in the dark, and not know I am a member of this church, you might be afraid of me. You might assume that I am Muslim, that I might have had something to do with the attacks, I might be an extremist. You know me, you know my husband, my children. You know I am about much more than what I look like on the outside; I am your fellow congregant, a Christian, a friend.

What I am saying is, it is important to take that chance – to get beyond the cover, and read that book."

While Victoria may have eased the minds of many who were in the church that evening, there were still many others, inside and outside the church, who were following a path of fear and ignorance; people who prejudge immigrants, particularly immigrants from the Middle East - especially Muslims.

When the word of her successful speech had spread throughout the church community, Victoria was asked to deliver similar seminars at other churches.

One of the churches where she went to talk was a local Lutheran Church. The congregation embraced her, and when they did, this opened a door that would bring her mission to a much higher level.

CHAPTER 29
"HER VOICE OF FAITH"

It was almost evening, and Victoria lovingly smoothed a white linen table cloth on each of the long fold-up tables. As she smoothed the creases, she reflected on how far she had come. She and a diverse community would celebrate Easter, and Victoria was eagerly preparing for their festive gathering. As she worked, she thought back on all that had happened. No longer was she alone in the mission.

Leaders at the Lutheran Church had joined with Victoria to begin the mission society, "Voice of Faith." Other churches wanted to know more about Islam, the culture of the Middle East, and how to show love to immigrants – especially how to love Hindus, Sikhs and Muslims. What "voice" could the churches use to show the love of God to people trying to make a new home in America? Silence was not an option.

The Voice of Faith had prospered. This was now more than a one-person mission; it was a community of voices - voices of faith.

Victoria was kept busy traveling inside and outside Florida, witnessing to new immigrants, especially the Muslims, Sikhs and Hindus. She also had the chance to encourage churches to reach out to these new ethnic groups. William went with her whenever he could.

For the past several years, they had ministered to churches in the Pompano and Fort Lauderdale areas, speaking with the immigrant populations, as well as the members of those churches. She found immigrants to minister to by frequenting the local ethnic food stores, and inviting them to a Bible study at a nearby apartment rented by Voice of Faith. This grew into something more.

In Southern Florida, it is not easy for women from the Middle East to purchase clothing they were used to. Voice of Faith began a sewing circle made up of women from all ethnic groups; they sewed brightly colored Middle Eastern apparel – and talked with each other. The immigrant women had many questions about American culture. Those who were interested in religious matters could join a Bible Study.

In both groups, Victoria tried to help ease the assimilation process. She would discuss other cultures and faiths, encouraging everyone to share where they were from, and what they believed, to educate the students about each other's culture.

Many people, Hindus, Sikhs, Christians and Muslims looked at the sewing circles and Bible studies as zones of comfort, as they labored to find their way in a new land.

The local Lutheran Church to which she and William belonged helped them establish a base on the West coast of Florida. Each month, a diverse group there gathered for Bible Study and social interaction. Victoria never felt more welcomed, more accepted, than she did among this multi-ethnic group.

As she prepared the tables, she thought more about her life. Her faith had helped her through many difficult moments; her faith had never left her, even when, at times, she had chosen to abandon it. When she felt troubled, she knew she could turn to Scripture and be set back on God's true path. As she thought of her faith life, she couldn't help but think of her friend Raj, and his faith journey.

✦

Little frustrated Victoria more than long delays at airports. She was shuffling to find a place in one of the uncomfortable, poorly padded seats at the gate, when she had to fumble to retrieve her ringing cell phone. It was signaling from a place deep inside her coat pocket.

"No, I am still waiting," Victoria told William. Their conversation was brief, and she promised to call him once she'd landed in Toronto. She was on her way to visit friends of theirs from the Presbyterian Church. Now she was stuck in a four-hour airplane delay.

Overhearing her conversation with William, a very light skinned, older, Middle Eastern man put a gentle hand on Victoria's shoulder. "You speak excellent Punjabi," he said to her, using the language himself.

Victoria was startled, but she couldn't help but smile. The man looked to be in his late seventies; his eyes were soft, gentle and intelligent. He spoke excellent Punjabi, but he dressed like an American. In fact, he was from Canada.

"You remind me of my mother," the gentleman said. "My name is Raj," and he stuck out his hand for Victoria to shake. She did, and introduced herself. Delayed by travel, they went together for a cup of coffee.

From that point on, what could have been an unbearable four-hour delay became a joyful experience. Victoria learned that Raj was from the same village in Punjab that her grandmother was from, and they eagerly shared stories about their time growing up in Pakistan.

"Tell me about you. What do you do in the United States?" Raj asked, leaning back in his seat.

"I help a group of immigrant women assimilate to the culture through conversation and Bible study."

"You're a Christian. I didn't expect that."

"Because I am from Pakistan?" The familiar anger that in the past would have accompanied a misjudgment about Victoria, this time did not appear.

"I was wrong to assume," Raj said apologetically.

"You are Hindu I presume?" Victoria asked.

"Now you are the one who is wrong to assume. I am an atheist."

Victoria laughed. Embarrassed, she said, "I owe you an apology. I've never met an atheist from India, since India has so many gods."

"Do you think differently of me now that you know?"

"No, I just feel badly that you've not welcomed the love of God into your life. I imagine that would be lonely."

"I'm quite happy, actually."

"You would be happier if you welcomed Christ into your life."

"I'm certain that's not true."

"How can you be so sure?"

"I saw the hatred, the violence and the chaos that the worship of God brought to Pakistan and the rest of the Middle East. If that's what believing in God would bring into my life, I am better off not believing."

Victoria thought she saw a haunted look in his eyes; she understood the terror of the atrocities he'd seen. Though she didn't agree, she could understand why Raj felt the way he did about religion and belief in God.

"If you read the words of Jesus, and start to live them, you'd feel much differently. His words lead you to a life of hope, of love. It's miraculous, and it's none of those horrible things you and I have both witnessed. I lived it too. I could have stopped believing, but I have remained a Christian all my life. The words of the Bible brought enough hope and peace into my life; the Holy Spirit of God helped me through the horrors of oppression."

"You're a good salesperson, Victoria," Raj laughed. "Send me your Bible. I will let you know what I think."

Victoria sent Raj a copy of the Bible as soon as she returned home. She, William and Raj maintained a long-distance friendship over the course of many years – talking on the phone, writing to each other. During those years, Victoria shared the good news of God's love with her elderly friend, seemingly without effect. Eventually, she heard from him no more.

One day, a card arrived in their mailbox. She saw the return address was from Raj. She opened the envelope. How was their friend doing?

In his familiar handwriting, Raj had written on a thick, white card: "I've finally discovered that you have been following the right path. Your God is the light and the way. And now, I've accepted Christ as my Savior too."

Victoria rushed inside and shared the news with her husband.

William smiled and placed an arm around his wife.

"You are a very convincing woman, Victoria. Once you begin speaking to someone about your faith, one cannot help but listen. You have a powerful voice, my dear."

A few months later, Victoria and William received another card; the address was his, but the handwriting was not Raj's. It was from the daughter of a friend of Raj. The news was not as joyful this time. She told them that Raj had passed away, but his transition had been peaceful; he had the love of Christ in his heart.

⚔ ⚔

Victoria lit an extra votive candle in Raj's memory and placed it in a special place on the table set for the evening's Easter celebration.

If given the opportunity, she would talk about him at today's celebration. While Victoria may have shown Raj the path to find his true faith, in that first conversation, long ago, he had given her a gift: the courage to talk about her faith openly. Since that time, she had used her voice to speak about the Lord, with all the zeal and love the Holy Spirit sparked within her.

She placed a bowl of piping hot *daal* on the table next to a platter of *naan* bread. She was so looking forward to the feast that was spread out to share with the different ethnic groups of Voice of Faith. After so many years of silencing her voice, Victoria felt free to speak out and express the wonderful Grace of God that had been given to her. She was eager to gift everyone with the knowledge she'd gained through her life, especially the difficult times.

Members of Voice of Faith began to trickle in. Victoria welcomed each with a broad smile and loving hug. Each woman brought a dish that represented her culture. Together they marveled at what they'd offered one another.

Maria brought a Spanish rice dish full of peppers and chorizo sausage. While she was a Christian from Cuba, she'd come to America and married a man from Pakistan.

"I am always pleasantly surprised at the generosity this group provides."

"Nothing can generate the feelings of nostalgia like food," laughed another woman of faith, Nadia, from Turkey. She was a Muslim who had immigrated to the United States in the late 1980's. Her contribution of coconut Kulucheh cookies to the table was met with murmurs of appreciation from the other women.

Victoria opened the gathering with a prayer of thanksgiving.

The Voice of Faith women ate and talked at the table Victoria had prepared.

"Afzal has begun to date," Nadia commented, her hands wrapped around her cup of coffee. Afzal was her sixteen-year-old son whom she'd been concerned with, as he'd shown no interest in dating up to this point.

"Wonderful! Have you met the lucky young lady?" Victoria asked.

Nadia rolled her eyes. "She's American. Blond hair, blue eyes. His father is beside himself."

"What did he expect?" Maria interjected.

"I suppose we both thought Afzal would remain true to the Muslim faith. We thought he was waiting for the right girl with the right values to come along." Nadia shook her head. "I guess we were wrong."

"It would be like finding a needle in a haystack," said Claudia, another Voice of Faith member. "Impossible."

"Is she Christian?" Victoria asked.

"Probably," Nadia replied. "It doesn't seem as if she's devout. Nevertheless, a Christian girl is not a good match for Afzal."

"Why not?" Victoria asked. "Do you know anything about her other than the fact that she's blond and she's probably a Christian?"

"That's enough. American values are vastly different from those in our Muslim culture."

"They are just different," Victoria said. "

"In my own life, I have tried to learn the lesson that my grandfather taught me as a young girl in Pakistan: our love for each other should transcend religion. Most of my life, I was persecuted and insulted by Muslims because I was Christian. Then, for the promise of a better, safe life, I moved to a foreign land. Now, even here, only to be insulted because I was Pakistani; people assumed I was Muslim because of where I was from. I've had many stumbles along the way as I tried to overcome hate with Jesus' love and forgiveness. And once I did that, I was finally able to see what my grandfather meant."

"And we are grateful," Claudia said. "It wasn't until Victoria and Voice of Faith spoke at our church that I became truly interested in learning about Eastern Religions, and cultures. I had my own ideas about Muslims, and "I didn't know all that I didn't know." I am more aware of other religions, and I try to accept them with love and respect. This group has helped me grow in many ways."

"I had my own perceptions about America and Christianity," Nadia admitted. "And through Voice of Faith I became awakened to the teachings of Christianity and what it is all about. I realized that we are so much more alike than we are different. I have to relearn that lesson every day."

"Thank you so much. I am so thankful that we've been blessed to come together this holy day." Victoria's eyes misted over with tears of joy. "I am grateful we've been able to look beyond our religions and our cultural differences and establish trusting and loving relationships.

Most of all this Easter, I am thankful for the Bridge God sent to us – Jesus. He is a bridge from this life to eternity – He is the bridge of love between people. By God's grace we will carry these things with us, not just for ourselves, but for everyone."

"Fine," Nadia said, slapping a palm on her thigh. "I'll give the blond American Christian girl a chance." The members of the group roared with laughter.

To Victoria, this meal was an affirmation, almost a culmination, of the path on which the Lord had led her. This was like the banquet God sets for His family every day in heaven. How often had people of such different ethnic backgrounds joyfully come together on earth to celebrate God's victory over death and the grave?

This was a table Talib could enjoy.

"You have heard that it was said, 'Love your neighbor, and hate your enemy.' But I tell you this: Love your enemies, and pray for

those who persecute you. In this way you show that you are children of your Father in heaven. He makes his sun rise on people whether they are good or evil. He lets rain fall on them whether they are just or unjust. If you love only those who love you, do you deserve a reward?"

Matthew 5:46 GWT

Made in the
USA
Middletown, DE